Pirates
and Lost Treasure of
COASTAL MAINE

GREG LATIMER

Published by The History Press
Charleston, SC
www.historypress.com

Copyright © 2020 by Greg Latimer
All rights reserved

The cover illustration depicts Dixie Bull, known as Maine's first pirate (*left*), locked in sword combat with the heroic fisherman Dan Curtis (*right*) as Curtis defends the Pemaquid colony from plunder. The illustration is based on a ballad written in the 1600s and sung by generations of Bristol fishermen that describes Curtis's slaying of Dixie Bull, thereby saving the colony from loss of all their goods. Both the ballad and the illustration could be described as "fanciful," as opposed to "historically accurate." In fact, Bull successfully raided Pemaquid, although it is unclear what was taken and if it had any value. Bull did suffer a casualty in that action. As his crew was pulling away from the colony in a small boat, a colonist identified as Curtis fired a shot, killing the first mate of the pirate crew. Also on the fanciful side are the circular fort and nearby fort house depicted in the illustration. Those structures were built some years after Bull's raid, and the fort house as well as a replica fort still exist at the present-day Colonial Pemaquid State Historic Site. *Cover image by Glenn Chadbourne.*

First published 2020

Manufactured in the United States

ISBN 9781467141000

Library of Congress Control Number: 2020930478

Notice: The information in this book is true and complete to the best of our knowledge. It is offered without guarantee on the part of the author or The History Press. The author and The History Press disclaim all liability in connection with the use of this book.

All rights reserved. No part of this book may be reproduced or transmitted in any form whatsoever without prior written permission from the publisher except in the case of brief quotations embodied in critical articles and reviews.

Dedicated to my grandchildren, Sol and Elle, Owen and Nora. Natural-born pirates, they are. Seeking all of the adventure their lifetimes will have to offer.

CONTENTS

Acknowledgements 7
Introduction 9

1. Pirates, Privateers and Wreckers 11
2. Pirate Politics and Practices 13
3. Dixie Bull, Maine's First Pirate 15
4. Tales of Captain Kidd in Maine 27
5. Pirate Treasure in Machias 49
6. Bartholomew Roberts's Treasure in Phippsburg 60
7. Disaster and Disappointment for Black Sam Bellamy's Crew 85
8. Pirate Deceit and a Massacre at Fort Loyall 95
9. Rachel Wall, Female Terror of the Stormy Seas 101
10. Pirate Weapons and Tactics 106
11. Plenty of "Piratitude" in Modern-Day Maine 120

Bibliography 125
About the Author 128

ACKNOWLEDGEMENTS

Whenever researching history, the author relies heavily on previously published works and documents. When working to write such history in a factual yet entertaining style, the author relies on the keen eyes and sharp wits of proofreaders. All of these elements, blended into a working manuscript, are what enabled this rendering of *Pirates and Lost Treasure of Coastal Maine*.

First and foremost in this effort was my wife, Sally, who has patiently, and lovingly, encouraged most aspects of my writing and discouraged, for good cause, others. This is the third book that Sally has been a participant in creating, and it is safe to say that all three of these projects would have been the lesser without her help.

Long ago historic scribes—Captain Chaloner Ogle and officers of the HMS *Swallow*, who so faithfully recorded the fight with Bartholomew Roberts in 1722; Captain Francis Champernowne, who, shortly after the fact, documented the Dutch conquest of Maine's Acadia area in 1889; and Fannie Eckstom and Mary Smyth, who included the ballad of Dixie Bull in their 1927 book *Minstrelsy of Maine*—helped preserve a part of history so that we can study it today. Even "Captain Charles Johnson," who is credited with writing *A General History of the Robberies and Murders of the Most Notorious Pyrates* in 1724 (for which the true authors are likely Daniel Defoe, Nathaniel Mink and possibly others), deserves some credit for contributing to pirate history. Even though much of the book is derived from questionable sources, *General History* drew readers and eventually created skeptics, driving them to conduct the first factual efforts at pirate research.

Acknowledgements

As more accurate information on piracy began to surface, cutting through the fiction perpetrated by attractive legends, a new kind of historical investigator emerged.

Ken Kinkor, who worked with Barry Clifford on locating the wreck of the pirate ship *Whydah* in Massachusetts, used insurance claims filed by the owners of vessels captured by Black Sam Bellamy to accurately track his voyage.

Benerson Little, a former Navy SEAL, uses his military experience to enhance his descriptions in *The Sea Rover's Practice: Pirate Tactics and Techniques*, as well as a number of other titles under his name.

David Cordingly, with his background as an English naval historian, ferrets out the hard facts and small details that bring pirates of the past to life for the modern-day reader.

James L. Nelson uses his creative drive and insatiable curiosity, combined with his background as a seafarer (including on square-rigged sailing vessels) to create fiction that is closely aligned with actual history.

Localized sources should not be forgotten.

Phil Di Vece, a resident of Wiscasset, Maine, used his superior local knowledge to discern fact from fiction in "Capt. Kidd's Pot of Gold Wasn't at the Rainbow's End," published in the *Wiscasset Newspaper*, a hometown weekly.

Finally, an author who combines both local knowledge and painstaking historical research is Maine native Colin Woodard, who wrote the incredibly well researched and definitive book *The Republic of Pirates*.

Many additional thanks to my excellent proofreading team, Michael and Lynne Borland, who are not only the most detail and style-oriented copyeditors I have ever worked with but also are very much modern-day pirates themselves.

Lastly are the Pirates of the Dark Rose reenactment group, who taught Sally and me the finer points of discharging historic artillery pieces, loading and firing flintlock firearms, swinging large edged weapons about (safely) and generally displaying "piratitude." Among this group are George Grey and his wife, Joanie, whose historic weapons collection was used in photos that illustrate this book.

Of course, I would like to acknowledge the often patient efforts of my commissioning editor, Mike Kinsella of The History Press/Arcadia Publishing, and the rest of the team there that brought this work to print.

INTRODUCTION

Fact and fiction…Two words that would seem to have the same line of separation as oil and water. Yet, as history is recorded, these words seem to blend in the telling, especially when it comes to pirates.

This book tries to separate the two and still tell a good yarn, because factual pirate history is even more interesting than all the fantastic tales told and told again over the last several hundred years.

In this book, I endeavor to establish a new level of understanding for piracy of times past, as well as a focus on pirates who cruised Maine waters and treasure they may have left behind, all based on as much historical fact as we can establish. We'll follow some of these pirates on their journeys before and after they visited Maine to gain perspective on their stories.

The reader will note an emphasis on attribution as part of my effort to establish factual elements and a thorough bibliography at the end of this book. I hope to lead those who open this volume on a well-researched adventure of discovery through these pages.

A poster for *The Black Pirate*, a 1926 movie starring Douglas Fairbanks and Billie Dove, depicting piracy in a highly romanticized way—a far cry from actual life on a pirate vessel. *Library of Congress.*

1
PIRATES, PRIVATEERS AND WRECKERS

Seaborne robbers came under a number of definitions during the era of buccaneer explorers in the 1600s and the so-called Golden Age of Piracy in the 1700s. The meaning of these terms is important for any reader of pirate history to understand.

Pirates were men, and sometimes women, without a nation, who saw fit to prey on any ships they could capture, regardless of national origin. They followed no rules, except for the ones they imposed on themselves. Pirate crews often shared their spoils in nearly equal amounts under agreements, known as articles, established before the voyage. More about this system is described in chapter 2, "Pirate Politics and Practices."

Some examples of well-known pirates include Blackbeard, Calico Jack Rackham and Edward Low. Pirates mentioned in this book include Black Sam Bellamy, Black Bart Roberts and Dixie Bull.

Privateers were essentially legal pirates, at least for the country that sponsored them. Sea rovers would approach a friendly government official, seeking a letter of marque, which gave them legal authority to take ships of the nationality specified in the letter. For instance, an English captain could apply to his government for a letter of marque to take French shipping, especially when the two countries were at war. Of course, if this captain were to be captured by the French, he would be considered a pirate.

The letter of marque would specify what share of the plunder would be paid out to the sponsoring government upon termination of the privateer's voyage. The balance would then be shared with the captain and crew.

Well-known privateers (some of whom may be historically misidentified as either pirates or naval captains) include Sir Francis Drake (licensed by the English), Jean Lafitte (licensed by Cartagena, now Colombia) and Samuel Tucker of Maine (licensed by U.S. Congress during the Revolutionary War and the War of 1812). Tucker is said to have taken more British guns and men than any other U.S. commander, including the Continental navy.

Privateers mentioned in this book include the well-known Captain William Kidd, who many people believe was a pirate.

Wreckers come as a whole different type of sea rover and can be subdivided into two categories: wreckers who caused ships to run aground, and wreckers who scavenged goods from the beaches or shallow water near where ships accidentally sank.

Sir William Phipps, who established the town of Phippsburg in Maine, earned his early fortune as a wrecker recovering treasures from sunken Spanish ships near the island of Hispaniola (modern-day Dominican Republic/Haiti), acting as an agent for the English Crown, a privateer of sorts.

Wreckers who waited on shore to prey on passing ships, using false signal lights at night to lure them into catastrophe on rocky headlands, may be regarded as the worst kind of criminals. In order to keep their crimes secret, they would commonly murder any sailors who survived the wreck. They would scramble over the decks and through the holds of grounded vessels, taking anything of value, usually operating in remote locations under cover of darkness. These shoreline scoundrels were careful in covering their identities, so there are no well-known names to share with this category.

Rachel Wall, who is featured in this book for a number of crimes, was a wrecker, operating off southern Maine in the Isles of Shoals with her husband and gang of cutthroats.

It is hoped that outlining these definitions will allow the reader a clearer concept of the sea rovers that visited Maine and perhaps left hidden treasure ashore.

2
PIRATE POLITICS AND PRACTICES

A vessel at sea is a community confined in a small space, floating—sometimes precariously—on water, surrounded by an endless ocean. For many pirates, most of them men without a nation, those seaborne communities served as their own sovereign state.

One might be surprised to learn that on some pirate ships there was a clearly defined democracy in effect.

While there were certainly some vessels in the firm command of a bloodthirsty tyrant, there were also a considerable number of pirate ships run by a pure democracy during the Golden Age of Piracy in the early 1700s. These voyages began with the ship's crew signing articles outlining the share out of loot at the end of the trip and some buccaneer "workman's compensation." Before the final share out, rovers who lost an eye or a limb would be paid an amount previously agreed upon by the crew through the articles.

Every member of the crew, regardless of ethnic or geographic origin, would have an equal vote on the ship, whether for immediate tactical purposes or long-range plans. Captains were voted in or out, without bloodshed, according to a tally of the crew that could be called for at any time, except in the heat of battle.

This system of "one person, one vote" was common to pirates and must have been of interest to American colonists at the many East Coast ports where the rovers often traded openly. The English parliamentarian system favored landowners and nobility. On a pirate ship with an agreement of articles, everyone aboard was essentially equal. To reflect this equality, and to avoid particular attention to any individual crew member in the event of capture, signatures on many of these articles were placed in a circular pattern.

Another surprise to the reader might be that many pirates used only as much violence, or threat thereof, as was required to capture the valuable cargo. Pirate crews were generally large, often crowded on a small but fast ship. They would come alongside the merchant vessels they were stalking and "vapor," a practice in which the sea rover crew, armed to the teeth, would loudly threaten the much smaller and lightly armed sailors aboard the commercial vessel.

Oftentimes, this vaporing, accented with a black pirate flag waving from the rigging—perhaps emphasized further with a cannon shot across the target's bow—would be enough to cause the merchantman to strike sails and heave to. Once captured, the merchant crew would often be given a choice to join the sea rovers or be set adrift in a small boat.

While certainly there were homicidal cutthroats also preying on merchant fleets, most pirates found that threatening their way into capturing cargo was much easier than bloody confrontations. A good example of a well-known pirate, who historically has been portrayed as a maniacal murderer, is Blackbeard, who although threatening by appearance and demeanor, is never recorded to have personally taken a single life until his final battle in the Ocracoke Inlet of North Carolina.

It is hoped that the little-known insights listed here will allow the reader a clearer perception of historic piracy as we explore the world of pirates of coastal Maine.

3

DIXIE BULL, MAINE'S FIRST PIRATE

"When the legend becomes fact, print the legend," is a timeless journalistic quote from the epic 1962 movie *The Man Who Shot Liberty Valance* with James Stewart, John Wayne and Lee Marvin. While that film is a western, the same sentiment can apply to some tales of piracy, in particular the story of Dixie Bull, who is Maine's earliest known pirate.

The pirate's tale, both legendary and factual, has been embraced by residents and visitors of Maine. Bull has been immortalized in print and celebrated in song.

So, as promised in the introduction of this book, I will do my best to separate fact from fiction, which won't be too hard in this case, as the limited amount of facts are fairly clear. Then we can get on with the colorful legend, including tales of hidden treasure.

For facts about Dixie Bull, we'll rely primarily on Maine author James L. Nelson, who is perhaps the foremost expert on this Down East buccaneer. (In the past, he even performed costumed and in character as the dread pirate.) Information attributed to Nelson is gleaned from a guest blog he did for mainecrimewriters.com in 2013 and from numerous personal conversations.

"Being the first pirate in Maine is akin to being the first vegetarian in Wyoming," Nelson wrote. "It's an interesting distinction but you are not exactly at the vanguard of a great movement. There are, however, a number of interesting aspects to Dixie Bull's life and legacy: a) he was Maine's first pirate, b) he's the only Maine pirate that most Mainers can name, and c) he really wasn't much of a pirate."

According to Nelson's research, Dixie Bull was born in the early 1600s in eastern England, where he apprenticed as a skinner and joined the Skinner's Guild. The guild had a monopoly that controlled the fur trade in England, which may be why, around 1630, Bull set sail for the Maine coast, believing a fortune could be made trading European goods with the Native Americans for beaver pelts that he could bring back to England.

"Such legitimate activity was hardly the stuff of pirates," Nelson noted. "Starting out as a legitimate trader was not exactly *de rigueur* when it came to the 'Sweet Trade'." However, Bull's status as a legitimate trader was to take pretty rough hit from a group of fellows who, predating Dixie Bull, may have really been the first pirates in Maine, but never well documented.

In June 1632, Bull was underway along the Maine coast trading with the Native Americans in a small vessel called a shallop when he was attacked by a boatload of Frenchmen, who robbed him of his goods and money.

With the shallop, and likely a sword, being the last things of value in his possession, Bull decided to take advantage of these remaining assets to seek out his attackers and retrieve his goods, or the value thereof. If he was unable to locate the French pirates who robbed him, he decided any French prizes would do.

First, he had to recruit a crew of like-minded sailors whom he could pay off with a share of the prizes. He set a southerly course, visiting coastal villages, possibly all the way to Boston, and acquired a crew of around fifteen scoundrels. He then set sail on a course north by east toward present-day Canadian waters in search of French prey.

The vengeful Bull and his crew found only a vast and empty ocean, devoid of French shipping. Running low on supplies, Bull decided to target any vessel he could take and captured several small trading ships, setting off alarms throughout coastal New England. A letter was sent to Governor John Winthrop of the Massachusetts Bay Colony that read, "Dixy [*sic*] Bull and fifteen more of the English, who kept to the east, were turned pirates."

Bolstered by the newly acquired supplies, Bull now became emboldened in pursuit of making up for his losses and reckoned if the only available prey were the possessions of other Englishmen, then that would have to do. He decided to target the coastal village at Pemaquid, which had been prospering through fishing and trade with the Native Americans.

Pirates and Lost Treasure of Coastal Maine

Right: Author James L. Nelson portrays Maine's first pirate, Dixie Bull, during a past event at Colonial Pemaquid State Historic Site in Pemaquid Harbor, where the pirate is said to have raided in 1632. *Author photo*.

Below: Performing in his past role as Dixie Bull, Maine's first pirate, author James L. Nelson discusses the replica of Fort William Henry, located behind him on the premises of Colonial Pemaquid State Historic Site. *Author photo*.

Left: These two historical reenactors, Ken Hamilton (*left*) and Gus Konitzky, portray the Native American and colonist elements active at Colonial Pemaquid. *Author photo.*

Below: The cemetery at the Colonial Pemaquid State Historic Site, with some headstones dating back hundreds of years. *Author photo.*

The village consisted of about eighty-five families, with their only fortification being a flimsy wooden palisade. Bull came ashore with a well-armed landing party and met with only weak resistance until after the pirates had loaded up about five hundred pounds of loot, torched the buildings and were rowing back to their ship. Someone on shore fired a musket shot that found its mark with Bull's first mate, killing him, and probably causing the pirates to lean into their oars with a bit more effort in order to gain the cover of their ship. (According to local legend, this shot was fired by a fisherman named Daniel Curtis, who was also credited in a popular, and legendary, ballad with killing Bull in swordfight.)

All along the coastline, fear spread over the "dread pirate" Dixie Bull. The governor hastily mustered a squadron of vessels to seek out Bull and his crew; but aside from a ship out of Salem captured by Bull, there were no other reports of piracy, and factual stories about Dixie Bull faded from the record. However, the legends still persist, including tales of hidden treasure, and the aforementioned ballad: "The Slaying of Dixie Bull." (Bull's first name varies between "Dixie" and "Dixey" in a number of texts. For this book, we use "Dixie" because Nelson's research indicates this to be the most accurate version. We use the name "Dixey" for the ballad because that is how it was published in the 1927 book *Minstrelsy of Maine*, which provided the following copy of the song.)

That ballad, written in the 1600s and sung by generations of Bristol fishermen, could be described as "fanciful," as opposed to "historically accurate." While a copy of the verse was located, the music for the ballad was not included in the book and may be lost to time.

The cover illustrator for this book, Glenn Chadbourne, who is also Stephen King's illustrator, used this ballad as the basis for the cover artwork showing the dread pirate Dixie Bull locked in mortal combat with Dan Curtis, the hero fisherman of Pemaquid.

It should be noted that in the text of this ballad, Pemaquid is referred to as "Jamestown," which was the correct term for the settlement at the time of Dixie Bull's raid—not to be confused with Jamestown in Virginia.

Also in the ballad, the fight takes place on Beaver Island, which is, in fact, located southwest of the colonial Pemaquid site, north of the larger Johns Island and can be seen from shore.

PIRATES AND LOST TREASURE OF COASTAL MAINE

THE SLAYING OF DIXEY BULL

Author unknown

*Dixey Bull was a pirate bold,
He swept our coast in search of gold.
One hundred years have passed away
Since he cast anchor in Bristol Bay.*

*Under the lee of Beaver's shore
He laid his craft three days or more;
He flaunted his flag and shot his lead,
Which kept the people out of bed.*

*Until the folks of old Jamestown
Had passed the word all around,
That Dixey Bull, the pirate bold,
Would not leave without their gold.*

*Into the fort the people came
To fight this man of bloody fame;
But well they knew the fort would fall
When stormed by powder and by ball.*

*Their gold was gathered in a pile
To send to him at Beaver's Isle,
So the pirate would go his way
And leave the waters of Bristol Bay.*

*But Daniel Curtis, a fisherman,
Feared not the flag from which they ran,
But took his skiff; bent to his oar
And rowed alone to Beaver's shore.*

*"I, Dan Curtis, my boat will pull
Down to the craft of Dixey Bull
And man to man, we'll meet tonight,
And settle for all in good fair fight.*

Pirates and Lost Treasure of Coastal Maine

*"And he who wins shall have the say
Of whether the riches go or stay;
If he kills me they're his by right,
If I kill him we win the fight."*

*The women wept, the children cried,
As he went off to the pirate's side,
He gave a roar and waved his hand,
And said, "I want to see the man.*

*"The captain of this bloody crew,
Then I'll tell him what I will do."
Bold was the pirate, Dixey Bull,
Said he, "Of fight I am chuck full.*

*"I'm the man your shores doth haunt;
Blood or your gold is what I want.
I will bleed for my country's sake
And for the gold put up a stake.*

*"Then single handed you and I
Shall fight until the other die."
Then Daniel Curtis rose and said,
"All right till you or I am dead."*

*The captain yelling, with a sneer,
Said, "With a sword no man I fear."
Accepts the challenge with a smile
And points his finger to Beaver Isle.*

*The people held their breath and prayed,
Because of Bull they were afraid.
The pirate crew gave three times three,
For Dixey Bull, king of the sea.*

*Alone they went to the Island bleak,
And to each other did not speak,
They hunted for a spot all sound
And laid their coats upon the ground.*

Pirates and Lost Treasure of Coastal Maine

Down to the belt the fighters strip,
O'er the sod commenced to skip,
Touched their swords and gave a twist,
To test the strength of each other's wrist.

Dixey tries for Curtis' arm,
But the thrust went wild and did no harm;
Dixey feigned, jumps to the right,
Slashed at Curtis with all his might.

Curtis dodges; and stepping back,
Gives the pirate's sword a whack.
The pirate swung his broadsword low
But Curtis dodged the awful blow.

A cut now falls on Dixey's neck
And groans rise from the pirate's deck.
The people cheer their Daniel brave,
As he their gold is going to save.

Dixey Bull a new trick tried,
Laying deep his sword in Curtis' side,
But Curtis, brave as a man could be,
Laughed at their cheers of three time three.

Dan knows his blood is flowing fast,
Yet for quarter would not ask,
But looked his man straight in the eye,
He knows that he or him must die.

Curtis fought for cause that's right,
Dixey, because he liked to fight;
Then down went Curtis upon his knee,
The pirate's crew gave three times three.

Dixey raised his sword on high
Which flashed like lightning in the sky,
He thought his man was nearly dead,
So gave a sweep to cut his head.

Pirates and Lost Treasure of Coastal Maine

As Dixey's sword was falling down
Curtis sprang up from the ground
In front of him by many feet
Went Dixey's cruel deadly sweep.

Like a flash at him Dan went
And through his breast his sword was sent,
The blood gushed out warm, bright and red,
The pirate staggered and fell dead.

Then like a stream rushed Dixey's gore
O'er Beaver's bleak and rocky shore;
When they saw that the fight was done
The people cheered because they'd won.

Pirates, your flag and anchor pull,
For Curtis killed your Dixey Bull.
That's how Curtis won the day
And killed his man in Bristol Bay.

He saved the gold and saved the town,
And won a name of great renown,
The skull and cross bones which they flew
Was the dipped by the pirate's crew.

Their anchor was then weighed o'er rail,
And gentle winds then filled their sail,
While cannons rang and cheers were given
They left for good old Bristol's haven.

On another fanciful note, there are a number of reports regarding treasure allegedly buried by Dixie Bull.

Since Bull never captured much treasure, it is somewhat unlikely that he would have had any spare plunder to bury. Nonetheless, we've included these for your knowledge, and to some degree, your entertainment. After all, nothing spices up a walk along the Maine coastline like a treasure hunt.

Damariscove Island, about five nautical miles due south of Boothbay Harbor, is mentioned as one of Bull's choices for hiding his ill-gotten gains. This island is also reported to be a favorite anchorage and possible treasure

Pirates and Lost Treasure of Coastal Maine

This small building at the Colonial Pemaquid State Historic Site, erected with mud and wattle using the same methods colonists utilized, is an accurate rendition of the structures that housed whole families during the 1600s, when Dixie Bull prowled the area. *Author photo.*

drop for a number of other pirates. It's a great location for such activities, with a protected harbor and far enough from shore to avoid curious eyes. It is one of Maine's earliest sites of European activity, first as a fishing station in the early 1600s, then as a year-round farming and fishing community in the early 1900s.

Today it is unpopulated except for caretakers during the summer months from the Boothbay Region Land Trust, which owns and manages most of the island. The island is open to the public but is only accessible by private boat. The Boothbay Region Land Trust hosts occasional excursions to the island. More information on these trips may be found at bbrlt.org or 207-633-4818.

Cushing Island is another spot where Bull is said to have concealed treasure. The island is privately owned, and without a rental property to spend the night in, it is not easily accessible to the public. (The daily ferry stays for only thirty minutes between trips.)

Richmond Island, located about one mile south of Cape Elizabeth, is another location said to have been a site for a Dixie Bull stash of plunder. In 1855, a farmer plowed up twenty-one pieces of gold and thirty-one pieces of silver on the island. There are some who speculate that this was part of Dixie

Reenactors portraying shoremen (fish processors) at Colonial Pemaquid State Historic Site give visitors a living example of life at the colony during the early 1600s, when the pirate Dixie Bull raided the location. *Photo by Neill De Paoli.*

Bull's loot from the sack of Pemaquid, but why he would stash it instead of holding on to it makes no sense, as he was destitute to start with.

According to an article in the *American Journal of Numismatics* published in 1870, some of these coins were undated but were identified as being "from the realms" of the English sovereigns Queen Elizabeth, James I and Charles I—a period from 1558 to 1649. A number of these coins are presently in the possession of the Maine Historical Society. Coins for which a date could be discerned, according to the Maine Historical Society, were a gold twenty-shilling coin with a creation date of 1606 and a gold Charles I unite coin with a creation date of 1625. There are two silver coins from Richmond Island also in possession of the Maine Historical Society for which exact creation dates could not be discerned: a shilling dated circa 1583 and a Queen Elizabeth I coin dated circa 1558.

Some of the coins in possession of the Maine Historical Society may be viewed online at mainememory.net, artifact numbers 34716, 35594, 35595 and 35596. All of these coins apparently came from the farmer's 1855 discovery. The coins are not on public display at the Maine Historical Society but may be viewed after special arrangements have been made in advance.

Bull's known activities in Maine occurred about 1632, which of course postdates all of the coins mentioned, so the possibility exists that these could have been part of Bull's loot. The Maine Historical Society asserts that the coins may have belonged to an early settler on the island named Walter Bagnell, who was active there until 1631, when he was apparently killed by Native Americans. Bull's crew would have visited after—and without knowledge of—the incident.

The island has been owned by the Sprague family since 1913 and welcomes visitors there through the Sprague Corporation. The island is accessible only by private boat with a smaller boat or kayak to haul out on sandy areas appropriate for landing. (The island dock is private and not intended for public use.) Day visitors are restricted to the beaches, and for those wanting to stay overnight, there are four primitive campgrounds. Advance arrangements are required for camping, and more information may be obtained online at blackpointcorporation.com/ram-island/richmond-island.

It may be well to remember, should one decide to seek the perhaps still hidden treasure of the dread pirate Dixie Bull, that while legends are laced with fiction, they are often based on at least one or two actual facts. So, while the possibility of hidden loot may be improbable, the few basic facts documented by researchers like James L. Nelson appear to make it highly probable that indeed Dixie Bull, Maine's first recorded pirate, prowled the waters of coastal Maine and raided the village at Pemaquid before fading into the depths of history, and mystery.

4

TALES OF CAPTAIN KIDD IN MAINE

Captain William Kidd may be the best-known pirate of all times, and he is said to have buried treasure in more Maine locations than any other sea rover known to history. The problems with these so-called facts are: Captain Kidd wasn't a pirate (even though he was tried, convicted and hanged as one), and there is absolutely no evidence he was ever in Maine. In fact, there's very little evidence he was ever north of Boston.

So, as promised in the introduction to this book, we will do our best to separate Maine pirate facts from Maine pirate fiction, and in the case of Captain Kidd, the reader may find the true stories behind these tales actually more interesting than the fiction already so widely believed.

While Kidd most probably never visited Maine, stories about him and his treasure abound in the state. An internet search of "Captain Kidd Treasure Maine" nets over one million returns. We'll try to clear some of those up (but not a million).

First, we'll give the reader a brief overview of Kidd's career.

William Kidd was reportedly born circa 1654 in the Scottish seafaring town of Dundee along the Firth of Tay (a fjord-like body of water allowing access to the open sea). There are conflicting accounts of his family and childhood.

He returns to the historical record in 1689 as captain of a privateer, operating under the auspices of the British colony on the island of Nevis, located in the eastern Caribbean. Under their agreement with Nevis, Kidd's crew were not paid by the British colonists but authorized to extract whatever

William Kidd in a portrait by Sir James Thornhill. *Public domain.*

plunder they could capture from the French, who were at war with England. Kidd and his buccaneers wasted no time in taking the English colony up on the offer, proceeding on a southeasterly course to the nearby French colony on the island of Marie Galante, located south of Guadeloupe Island. According to reports, Kidd's crew sacked the only town on the island, making off with a ton of sterling for their effort.

Kidd then traveled north, where he received privateering commissions from the colonies of New York and Massachusetts Bay. It is at this point, in the early stages of his career, that Kidd may have wandered into the waters offshore of Maine, which were then part of the province of Massachusetts Bay. He may have taken a French privateer on this cruise, as well as other prey, but available records are sketchy. This cruise would have likely been during the fair-weather summertime months circa 1690.

In 1691, Kidd was spending the spring months in New York, where in May he was married to Sarah Bradley Cox Oort, a woman twice widowed who inherited a great deal of assets from her first husband, making her one of the richest women in New York. It may be surprising to some that Kidd was a well-respected member of New York society; he even helped build the first Trinity Church building on Wall Street, which is still holding services today. In 1696, according to church records, Kidd loaned the construction crew a "runner and tackle," a pulley system for hefting stones. Kidd may have become a regular churchgoer at Trinity if he had lived long enough. The church didn't open until 1698, while Kidd was at sea and then later in custody. He was executed in 1701. He had paid in advance to rent a family pew, which Kidd's heirs were able to continue enjoying some seventeen years after his execution.

Captain William Kidd's best known, and fateful, final voyage began in 1696. In an unusual investment scheme, a group of English lords met with Kidd in London to discuss a privateering voyage to the Indian Ocean intended to capture pirates and their ill-gotten goods and return the spoils to England, where the investors would take 10 percent of the treasure as their cut. After expenses, Kidd could split up the rest with his crew.

His privateering commission (known as a letter of marque) was signed personally by King William III.

He was outfitted with a new ship, the *Adventure Galley*, which was specifically purposed as a pirate hunter. As a galley, the ship was outfitted with two banks of long oars called sweeps that the crew could use to maneuver the vessel even on windless days, or when the wind direction was against them. The *Adventure*'s ship-rigged sail plan, three masts filled with square sails, allowed it to achieve a top speed of fourteen knots (sixteen miles per hour), which was considered fast at the time. Its thirty-four guns were carefully selected light artillery pieces, with the lower weight allowing for greater ship speed. Moreover, the guns weren't intended to sink ships, just disable them and allow the privateers to board and loot the vessels. Finally, the *Adventure Galley* was well staffed with a crew of 150, allowing for the loss of some crew members to illness or as casualties and still be battle ready.

However, the *Adventure Galley*'s first loss of crew members was to come in a completely unexpected way. In April 1696, the *Adventure Galley* weighed anchor and started down the Thames River to gain the open ocean, slowly making way around a bend in the river past the Isle of Dogs, when it approached a Royal Navy yacht. According to custom, Kidd was required to salute the naval vessel, usually by firing a charge without shot from one of his guns. When *Adventure Galley* failed to make the proper salute, the Royal Navy vessel fired a warning shot to force Kidd to comply. Instead of responding with a proper salute, Kidd's crew offered a special recognition to the naval officers; they lined up on the *Adventure Galley*'s deck, turned away from the yacht and slapped their backsides. (There are some reports that they may have dropped their trousers to reveal a wee bit more of their backsides, but these could not be corroborated.) This sort of disrespect caused the Royal Navy officers to add enough sail to their yacht to overtake and board the *Adventure Galley*, whereupon they forced much of the crew into Royal Naval service through a practice known as pressing.

With his crew already depleted even before leaving English waters, Kidd set a course west by south and arrived in New York on July 4, 1696, with the objective of bringing on more crew. However, the privateering offer Kidd was making to prospective crew members wasn't very enticing to these New York sailors, many of whom had already enjoyed the pleasures of pirating, where the loot was divided in nearly equal portions among the crew.

Under the privateering rules that Kidd was offering, crew members worked under a "no prey, no pay" arrangement. Moreover, crew would

In what may not be an entirely accurate depiction, Captain William Kidd is shown welcoming guests aboard the *Adventure Galley* in New York Harbor, apparently prior to departure for his pirate hunting venture in the Indian Ocean. *Painting by Jean-Léon Gérôme, public domain.*

have to wait until the end of the voyage and after the bills and the investors were paid before they received any money. All of that could mean a long and dangerous journey without any guarantee of payment, or the amount thereof. The only advantage to privateers was that, technically, it was legal—at least until someone in power decided otherwise or if they were captured by the people they were preying on.

Most pirates also had a fair amount of say aboard their vessels, with many issues being put up for a vote. Discipline on privateering vessels was in stricter military style, with officers in absolute command. Discipline on pirate vessels was essentially nonexistent without a vote of the crew.

The challenge of bringing on more crew, combined with the fact that Kidd could visit his family in New York, made for a long layover, and Kidd didn't leave New York until September 1696, arriving in the area of Madagascar in March 1697, where he suffered several setbacks.

Putting into a port known then as Johanna and now as Anjouan, popular with English ships, in the Comoros Islands group, Kidd sought to replenish his supplies. Local merchants declined his request for a line of credit. Still needing to perform some maintenance on his ship after the long voyage, Kidd traveled to a nearby island with tidal flats that would allow him to careen his vessel. Careening, sometimes known as "heaving down," was a process whereby a ship could be positioned over a sandy shoal that would leave it grounded on one side when the tide went out. The crew could then work on areas normally below the water line, scraping the hull free of sea growth and making structural repairs. When the next set of tides came, the other side of the ship could be repaired and cleaned. The crew was able to control which side of the ship would be exposed by affixing a line to the top of the ship's main mast and tying it off to a large tree or rock on shore, thereby weighting the "down" side of the hull and exposing the "up" side.

Kidd's choice of a careening location may have worked well for the maintenance process but had an unintended and tragic effect on his crew, when a virulent disease (reported by different sources as cholera, yellow fever or malaria) killed off an estimated one-third of their number. For the second time since the *Adventure Galley* left port, Kidd was faced with recruiting somewhere in the area of fifty new crew members.

His only option to find new crew was to return to Johanna, which turned out to be fortunate in another way, as his line of credit was now established and he was able to lay in provisions and replace gear.

By that time, members of Kidd's crew who had started the voyage in London were now a year into their journey and becoming restless. Aside from a French fishing boat taken on the Atlantic crossing, the *Adventure Galley* had yet to capture a lucrative prize.

Some of the crew, especially the former pirates recruited in New York, were also becoming frustrated with their captain's strict adherence to the legal confines of his letter of marque. He was restricted to taking only the plunder of "pirates, free-booters, and sea rovers," some of them even mentioned by name.

Perhaps more importantly, his royal investors were quite clear with Kidd about other potential prizes. A closing sentence in the letter of marque, gives a dire, if not prophetic, warning: "We do hereby strictly charge and command you, as you will answer to the contrary at your peril, that you do not, in any manner, offend or molest our friends or allies, their ships or subjects, by colour or pretence of these presents, or the authority thereby granted."

Part of the effect of this sentence meant that the only nationality Kidd could target would have been the French, with whom the English seemed to be constantly at war.

Pirates and Lost Treasure of Coastal Maine

In April 1697, Kidd was near Madagascar. He had filled out his crew, and all aboard were probably hopeful their luck was about to change. They made sail and pointed the *Adventure Galley*'s bow north by east, following the coastline on their port side up to the horn of Africa. Likely somewhere near twelve degrees north latitude, they changed to a westerly course, bound for the Bab el-Mandeb Strait, located near the Gulf of Aden between present-day Yemen to the north and Djibouti to the south. Here the *Adventure Galley* began pursuing pirates that were hunting for vessels full of pilgrims bound for Mecca carrying vast amounts of coin and valuables to pay for their pilgrimage or trade ships with lucrative cargo.

The passage through the Bab el-Mandeb Strait was (and continues to be) very narrow, only about twenty miles across. It remains, in modern times, a crossroads of international shipping interests and a highly strategic bit of real estate, at either border.

Most sea rovers operating in this environment at the time would send out flotillas of pirate vessels working by line of sight within several miles of one another, weaving a nautical net to capture any prize of their choice, with the plunder to be shared by the participating vessels.

However, Kidd was apparently unable to locate and capture any pirate vessels, and it is at this juncture that accusations of piracy began to arise.

The best-documented incident occurred in September 1697, many long months after the *Adventure Galley* and its treasure-hungry crew sailed from the Comoros. A large convoy of heavily laden merchant vessels from Mughal (part of present-day India) was making its way through the Bab el-Mandeb Strait. The ships' objective was the port city of Mocha (then known as Mocha Road), about fifty miles north of Bab el-Mandeb. The incident is described in detail by Richard Zacks in his well-researched book *Pirate Hunter: The True Story of Captain Kidd*.

Kidd and the *Adventure Galley*, apparently having some advance notice that the fleet would be arriving, were loitering in the area. Also in the neighborhood was the British East India Company ship *Sceptre* under the command of Edward Barlow. *Sceptre*'s mission included protecting British East India Company interests, and it was well appointed for the task, carrying a well-trained crew with forty guns at its disposal.

Kidd had cunningly positioned his ship behind one of the islands in the strait. He sent two men ashore to take up an elevated position on the island and use a signal flag to alert the *Adventure Galley* when they had spotted the fleet.

A number of days passed, with heat waves rolling off the nearby desert making conditions miserable, before the signal flag was finally waved one evening. Kidd recovered his shore party and stayed out of sight during the overnight hours, lying in wait.

The next morning, daybreak came with clear skies but calm winds. This was an advantage for the *Adventure Galley*, which could still make way using its long oars.

The *Sceptre* was also in the area, but still some distance away, when one of its lookouts reported to Captain Barlow that there was an unusual gap in the convoy formation. Barlow brought his spyglass to bear and observed a ship unfamiliar to him. The English captain astutely observed that the strange ship's sails were set in an odd manner, allowing it a range of tactical options. Having set two small topsails for steerage and easy maneuverability, the other, larger sails on the intruder were loosely furled so that they could be easily deployed, allowing the ship as much speed as possible for pursuit, or escape.

Barlow also noticed that only flag displayed on the ship was a broad, unmarked, red pennant. This was not a "no mercy" flag sometimes flown by pirates but instead intended to signal that the bearer was a superior ship, used to designate a commander's vessel or the lead ship in a convoy.

Aboard the *Sceptre*, Barlow perceived the unidentified vessel as a danger to the convoy he was tasked with protecting, but it was still out of cannon range. Barlow decided not to make sail in obvious pursuit of the distant ship, instead deciding to hold his position and appear as unthreatening as possible, allowing the target to unwittingly come to him. Barlow ordered a small number of his crew to make themselves busy on deck with routine chores, sending the rest of his "Jack Tars" below decks to ready the guns for action.

On the ships of the Mughal fleet, the officers and men were likely having a hard time deciding what the strange ship in their midst was up to. Since it seemed nonaggressive, they may have decided to leave it be until its intentions were clearer.

Aboard the mysterious ship, which was of course the *Adventure Galley*, Kidd was probably enjoying his access to the fleet. However, it was never established exactly what his purpose was. He may have been using his close-in tactics to seek out a lucrative merchant ship to plunder, or he may have postulated that such an attractive target as the convoy would be sure to lure predatory pirate vessels. Using the Mughal ships as mobile cover, he could surprise any pirate, once he showed his colors.

It was likely that he was warily watching the *Sceptre*, which at the time seemed to be sitting quietly and displaying no flag. The distance slowly closed between them as the mild winds tugged away on their sails. Perhaps it was finally a sea rover's ship—covered under Kidd's letter of marque—of the type he had been seeking for over a year, with holds full of stolen plunder.

Or, perhaps not. Aboard the *Sceptre*, Captain Barlow had quietly crewed and lowered two longboats. Using years of experience, he judged the distance between his ship and the unknown vessel that he perceived to be a pirate. "Seeing the pirate as near as he intended to come, being almost abreast of us, we presently hoisted our colours and let fly two or three guns at him, being well-shotted, and presently got both our boats ahead having very little wind, towing towards him," Barlow later reported.

Kidd must have been overwhelmed for some seconds, as he watched the English Jack hauled up the ship's rigging, heard and saw the guns fire directly on him, with the shot raising plumes of white water around his vessel, which was fortunately missed by the first hostile volley. Then, he would have seen the long boats come around and begin towing the well-armed warship ever closer to him.

The Mughal ships quickly caught on. Observing gunfire directed at the mystery ship, the gunners aboard several ships in the convoy sighted in on the target and engaged it with their own guns.

With cannonballs churning the water around him, some hitting his rigging, Kidd rolled out his guns and returned fire, targeting only the convoy vessels, striking one of them in the sail and at points above the waterline. Whether his ineffective fire was purposeful was never established. Of particular note, Kidd never returned fire on the *Sceptre*, not even training his guns in its direction.

Aboard the two long boats, the *Sceptre*'s crew members strained at their oars, trying to close range to gain a more effective firing position.

Kidd ordered his crew to the oars with which his galley-style vessel was well equipped. Gaining the open ocean first, he was fortunate to catch a breeze, likely deploying his furled sails, bringing the *Adventure Galley* clear of the convoy and gaining some distance.

The *Sceptre* continued in slow-motion pursuit until nightfall, then bore away back toward the fleet. Captain Barlow later noted that if the mystery ship had hostile intent, it could have easily targeted several heavily laden merchant ships and taken them before the *Sceptre* could have intervened. Nonetheless, there are charges published in some modern sources that this episode was proof that Kidd had turned to piracy and that he intended to take one of the Mughal vessels, in spite of evidence to the contrary.

The action at Bab el-Mandeb included several factors that were not only confusing but also common to the times. First was the reticence of some captains to clearly identify their ships and the purpose they were serving. Kidd never displayed any flag of nationality during the incident, and Captain Barlow on the *Sceptre* didn't raise his colors until the last minute. The apparent intent of both captains was to mislead the other in order to gain a tactical advantage, but the use of "false flags" was practiced widely during the period for many reasons. This practice was to have consequences for Kidd, both during his operations in the Indian Ocean and his eventual trial before the High Court of the Admiralty.

Another source of piracy accusations against Kidd came from the leaders of countries in the heavily traveled region of the northern Indian Ocean, where there were pirates aplenty. These leaders didn't speak English well, and many of the pirates had names that were challenging to pronounce in the native languages of the area. However, the one-syllable name "Kidd" was easy to pronounce, so perhaps it was confused with the actual names of other pirates in the complaints to the British East India Company that made their way back to London.

Leaving the Gulf of Aden, Kidd set an easterly course following the coastline of modern-day Yemen and then Oman before adjusting to a more southerly course making for the Malabar Coast of west India.

At this point, members of Kidd's crew, having never taken a valuable prize after more than a year at sea, were becoming mutinous. There had been a number of incidents where ships were boarded and deprived of some items they were carrying, but these were more acts of commandeering supplies than capturing treasure, although some valuables were taken. Some of these incidents could have certainly been considered piracy, depending on one's point of view. Nonetheless, as far as Kidd was concerned, he continued to follow the requirements outlined in his letter of marque. As his crew grumbled below deck, Kidd, ensconced in his captain's cabin, continued to make plans that would hopefully end in a legal capture.

In October 1697, somewhere off the Malabar Coast, a ship flying Dutch colors came within view of the *Adventure Galley*'s lookouts. A gunner named William Moore aboard Kidd's ship urged his captain to engage and take the ship, but Kidd refused, knowing the act would violate his letter of marque and certainly be considered piracy. An argument ensued, with Kidd calling Moore "a lousy dog."

"If I am a lousy dog, you have made me so," Moore replied in a rage. "You have brought me to ruin and many more," Moore added, referring

A fanciful illustration of Captain Kidd on the quarterdeck of *Adventure Galley*. *Howard Pyle, public domain.*

to the crew. Perhaps as crew members gathered closer, murmuring in agreement, Kidd decided he better take forceful action, so he heaved an iron-bound bucket at Moore, striking him square in the head. Moore fell, bleeding profusely from a fractured skull. He died the next day.

At the time, a ship's captain was allowed considerable latitude when disciplining a mutinous crew, and Kidd likely felt justified in his act. Later, not everyone would share that opinion.

In November 1697, the long wait for a legal capture was about to end. Kidd was short on rations and water but had nonetheless continued patrolling the Arabian Sea offshore of Callicut (modern-day Kozhikode on the southwest coast of India). Kidd's lookouts made out a sail on the horizon south of Sacrifice Rock (modern-day Velliyamkallu).

The early evening darkness was beginning to fall, but Kidd ordered men aloft to set more sail as he took a bearing on the distant ship. Night came, and Kidd held his bearing as his lookouts strained their eyes to keep track of the target's white sails, fading in and out of the darkness. All night long the *Adventure Galley* held its course, slowly gaining on the other ship.

When the sun rose, the *Adventure Galley*, flying under a false flag of white, denoting Royal France, had closed in on its prey. The other ship ran up French and Moorish colors but failed to ease off its course until Kidd fired warning shots across its bow. The target was the 150-ton ketch *Rouparelle*.

Kidd had a French-speaking member of his crew hail the ship and invite its officers aboard. According to crew members on the *Adventure Galley*, Kidd took up a hidden position while the French-speaking crewman asked to see the *Rouparelle*'s papers. When the captain produced French papers, Kidd stepped into view, exclaiming after his long voyage: "By God, I have got you! You are a free prize to England!"

After fourteen months at sea, Kidd had finally taken a legal prize. Or had he?

Kidd's crew was eager to claim their capture. They immediately took to a boat and boarded the ketch, quickly subduing the surprised crew.

Back on the *Adventure Galley*, circumstances were changing for the worse. Upon further investigation, Kidd discovered that the *Rouparelle* was an Indian-owned ship bearing Dutch cargo—allies of England. The French papers presented were simply a passport through the area, not an ownership document.

Kidd recalled his crew and addressed them on deck. His speech urging them to return the vessel and its contents to the owners was likely met with uproarious laughter, and the *Rouparelle*'s fate as a captured prize was final.

In spite of Kidd's concerns, according to the maritime laws of the day, the capture was legal, in the opinion of Kidd biographer Richard Zacks.

There wasn't much in the way of treasure on board. Two chests of opium, a dozen bales of cotton, fifty quilts and some personal possessions. Kidd's crew renamed their prize the *November* and sailed it to a nearby port to sell off the cargo for about £150, just enough to buy some provisions.

With his freshly loaded supplies and his two-ship flotilla, Kidd set sail in search of what hoped to be another legal capture, this time with a heavily laden treasure ship. He would also once again find himself in a confusion of flags, foreign papers and a mutinous crew desperate for profit.

In January 1698, Kidd's two-ship flotilla continued its patrol south along the western coast of India, nearing the southern tip of that country. At times, the vessels sailed together, other times well separated. Kidd used his consort vessel to scout and to make trips to shore for provisions. The coastwise shipping traffic was thick with merchant ships, but as his angry crew grumbled, Kidd passed up the many vessels not covered by his letter of marque.

On January 30, Kidd was aboard the *Adventure Galley*, operating alone while the *November* was off on some other mission. The *Adventure Galley* was about twenty-five leagues (approximately seventy-five miles) offshore of Cochin (also known as Kochi) when the crew spotted a large vessel traveling alone.

Kidd ordered more sail and went in pursuit of the vessel, raising a French flag to disguise his intentions. It took some four hours for Kidd to close enough distance to come within range of his spyglass. Training the instrument on the ship's rigging, Kidd saw that it was flying Armenian colors—not covered by his letter of marque—possibly a false flag. Perhaps now able to make out the name of the vessel as *Quedagh Merchant*, Kidd realized that the large ship was likely loaded with valuable cargo. Upon catching up with his target, Kidd ordered it to heave to. Heavily outgunned and outnumbered, the crew of the *Quedagh Merchant* quickly complied.

Kidd found a French-speaking member of his crew to order the captain of the *Quedagh Merchant* over to his ship. The merchantman's crew found its own French-speaking member and located a valid French pass among its papers. They provided him with the pass and sent him over in a boat, posing as captain of the *Quedagh Merchant*.

As soon as the "captain" stepped aboard *Adventure* with the French papers, Kidd ordered his crew to lower the French flag on his ship and run up English colors. The *Quedagh Merchant* emissary watched the ensign hoisted and turned to Kidd, reportedly saying, "Here is a good prize." It was that quick—and that simple. After almost two years on the prowl, Kidd finally found himself in possession of a real prize. A subsequent search of the *Quedagh Merchant* located a cargo of gold, silver, silks, satins, muslins and more East Indian merchandise. The cargo was estimated to be valued in the area of £50,000, which would result in doubling the investors' money upon return to England.

There was also a report that Kidd, poking around out of sight from the crew, located a locked chest in the captain's cabin that, once forced open, was found to contain a hoard of jewels. There are some reports that Kidd never revealed this find to his shipmates.

Unfortunately, other discoveries were made aboard the *Quedagh Merchant*. First, the real captain of the ship was located and found to be an Englishman. Second, it was discovered that much of the cargo was owned by Armenians, who were allies of England, and was being brokered by the English East India Company. In spite of the fact that the capture was technically legal, any interference with English East India Company trade would not sit well back in London. Kidd tried to explain this to his crew, but it was too late. They had been celebrating the capture (some reports describe five days of constant partying), and there was no convincing them to give up any of their newfound wealth.

What no one aboard the *Adventure Galley* knew was that a substantial portion of the cargo belonged to an Indian nobleman, a good friend of the grand mogul, who was closely associated with English East India Company.

The capture of the *Quedagh Merchant* was to end Kidd's long voyage. Although he failed to take any pirate vessels, *Adventure Galley* successfully captured a nominal prize in the *Rouparelle/November* and a lucrative prize in the *Quedagh Merchant*, both with legitimate French papers that Kidd now had in his possession.

Kidd sailed to Île Sainte-Marie and was somewhat surprised to see a large pirate vessel, the *Mocha Frigate*, anchored in the harbor. Now was his chance to take a pirate as prize, and he was confident the *Mocha Frigate*'s holds were full of loot. He gathered intelligence in the harbor that convinced him the *Mocha Frigate* and its crew were no match for the *Adventure Galley* and his privateers. As he gathered his crew to make the attack, they mutinied, not wanting to fight with their own brethren and tired of waiting to share out any treasure with Kidd, which would have to wait for a return to London. Some 115 of Kidd's crew took control of the *Adventure Galley*, leaving Kidd with around 15 or so loyal crew. Kidd gathered up his loyalists and left the ship to gather some backup from the rogues at Île Sainte-Marie. After some time, Kidd returned with a heavily armed group, including some Malagasy tribesmen. They retook the ship, but the mutinous crew had already removed a great deal of cargo, leaving it spread out on the beach and declaring they would finally see some kind of payday.

Kidd still had a goodly amount of treasure left behind by the looters, but he had to cool his heels in Île Sainte-Marie and keep the remaining loot safe for four months—until favorable winds were expected in October.

At this point, the *Adventure Galley*'s pumps could no longer keep up with water seeping into its hull due to damage caused by wood-eating worms, and the once proud vessel was rotting out from right under the crew's feet. Kidd transferred treasure and crew to the *Quedagh Merchant* and scuttled the *Adventure Galley* near Île Sainte-Marie. It is unclear what fate befell the *November*. The *Quedagh Merchant* was renamed *Adventure Prize*.

When the prevailing winds changed, Kidd was finally able to set a course toward the Cape of Good Hope and around the southern tip of Africa before turning to the north and home.

Kidd became aware at this time that English authorities might be seeking him as pirate, but he attributed this to some misunderstanding, confident his investors would support him. However, at some point, his confidence eroded, and Kidd ended up sharing out what was left of the treasure with what was left of his crew, somewhere near the present-day Dominican Republic, scuttling the *Quedagh Merchant/Adventure Prize* near the island of Santa Catalina on the northern coast of that country. (The wreckage of the *Quedagh Merchant/Adventure Prize* was located off Catalina Island in 2007. No treasure or valuables were located with it.)

Kidd held on to a substantial chest, likely filled with the most valuable and portable items, and made his way up the American coast to New York aboard a small sloop. He took an unlikely route in order to avoid any members of his former mutinous crew. He stopped first at Gardiners Island, near New York, where he buried his treasure chest for safekeeping and leverage. This was the only known occasion and place where Kidd actually buried treasure.

Upon arriving in New York City, Kidd sought out the colonial governor, Richard Coote, the First Earl of Bellomont, who was also one of Kidd's investors. Coote was in Boston, and upon receiving word from Kidd, invited the privateer captain to meet him there, luring him with promises of clemency. However, clemency was not to be for the unfortunate Kidd. He was immediately arrested on July 6, 1699, and taken to the Boston Gaol, also known as Stone Prison. Before his arrest, he had shared the location of

Pirates and Lost Treasure of Coastal Maine

An imagined illustration of Captain Kidd burying treasure with a number of his crew on a lonely shoreline. Kidd actually did bury treasure, without help from his crew, on Gardiner Island near New York City. It was recovered by the authorities immediately following Kidd's arrest. *Howard Pyle, public domain.*

his treasure on Gardiners Island with Coote, who immediately sent a group to recover it. He had also presented his French papers, the only solid proof that he took his two prizes legally, to Coote, who took them into his custody. After over a year at the jail, most of it in solitary confinement, Kidd was put in chains and placed aboard a London-bound ship.

Upon arrival in London, he was transferred to Newgate Prison, where he awaited trial before the High Court of Admiralty. When he was charged in court, he had two surprises: In addition to piracy, he was charged with the murder of William Moore, and his French papers had disappeared.

The outcome of his trial seemed preordained, with a verdict of guilty on all charges and a sentence of death by hanging. Upon delivery of his sentence, according to *A General History of the Pyrates*, Kidd protested to the court: "My Lord, it is a very hard sentence. For my part I am the innocentest person of them all, only I have been sworn against by perjured persons." He begged for his French papers as proof, but the papers were nowhere to be found.

In the end, there was no mercy for the privateer Captain William Kidd. On May 23, 1701, at Execution Dock, located on the bank of the Thames River in Wapping, Kidd's bad luck held right up to his moment of death. As was customary for the hanging of pirates at the time, Kidd was to be hanged with a short rope, which meant that instead of quick death—from his neck breaking at the terminal snap of a long rope—he would slowly strangle at the end of a short rope. But even this wouldn't be easy. When the gallows trapdoor dropped, the rope broke, leaving Kidd dazed but alive. Despite the pleas of some audience members that authorities observe the tradition that a broken rope was a sign from God and therefore cancels the hanging, another rope was found. Kidd was successfully, and horribly, strangled, as his body jerked in the "Marshal's Dance" while he slowly succumbed to asphyxiation. His body was then placed in a steel cage known as a gibbet. Gibbets were built in the shape of a man and used to put on display the body of a pirate in an elevated location such as Tilbury Point for all to see and so be forewarned of the cost of piracy. Or perhaps, in this case, it heralded the cost of becoming a pirate hunter for rich and powerful men.

The French papers from the *Rouparelle/November* and *Quedagh Merchant/Adventure Prize*, which could have acquitted Kidd of the piracy charge and had been dutifully turned over to Coote, seemed lost forever. As time went on, some historians began to wonder if they ever existed. Then, in 1910, an American treasure hunter named Ralph Paine was going through the archives of the English Board of Trade in London when he encountered

Captain Kidd's body gibbeted (placed in a steel cage) and put out for public display on the Thames River at Tilbury Point for all to see. *From* The Pirate's Own Book *by Charles Ellms, public domain.*

some aged documents that appeared out of place. Upon closer examination, he learned that he had discovered Kidd's long-lost French papers. Perhaps Kidd was, in fact, "the innocentest person of them all."

Once the life of Kidd the man had been ended, the story of Kidd the legend began—and with it tales of hidden treasure in Maine.

Perhaps the best-known tale of Kidd's treasure in Maine originates from Deer Isle, located on the eastern side of Penobscot Bay. This story is so resilient that it continues to be told as though it were truth and was recently featured as fact in several television documentaries. In fact, a producer for one of these so-called documentaries contacted a local source in Maine and, upon being told the Kidd story was fabrication, simply found other, more cooperative sources and aired the tale anyway.

The original perpetrator of this mistruth was industrialist, lawyer and banker Franklin Harvey Head, who apparently enjoyed writing tall tales with little regard for actual facts. He made his stories even more convincing by attributing his facts to combinations of nonexistent documents and invented quotes from human sources, including some well-known persons. He would also "copyright" his pieces for further authenticity.

He was able to afford printing his observations at will and was the publisher of his first book.

His motive for producing these far-fetched articles is unknown. Perhaps he felt they were humorous. Certainly, if he were still around, he would probably be laughing hysterically that so many people are still reading his work and some of them still believing it.

In 1887, he authored a hoax titled "Shakespeare's Insomnia and the Causes Thereof." He followed this in 1898 with a pamphlet that tells the Kidd story titled *Studies in American History: A Notable Lawsuit*. Its contents are entirely false, even though noted industrialist John Jacob Astor (the fourth) and Frederick Law Olmsted, a well-known architect, were "quoted" extensively. Head reportedly based his description on a conversation with Marion Olmsted, the daughter of Frederick Law Olmsted, an early settler on Deer Island.

In 1934, this tale was picked up by *Liberty Magazine* and published as completely factual under the title "Olmsted and Captain Kidd's Treasure."

The core of this manufactured story revolves around a nonexistent lawsuit alleged to have been filed by Olmsted claiming that John Jacob Astor (the first) discovered Captain Kidd's treasure on Deer Isle in a cave on property owned by Olmsted and that this treasure was so vast, that it provided Astor with his original fortune, allowing him to invest over $1 million in New York real estate, creating an empire. In the pamphlet, Olmsted was now suing Astor (the fourth) to recover the original amount and all that it had earned over the years.

According to Head's story, the trail to Kidd's treasure on Deer Isle began at Kidd's sentencing in London. After the court decreed that he should be sentenced to death and he was being led away, he whispered to his wife and handed her a small piece of paper, upon which were scribbled the numbers 44106818. The court officials, noticing this handoff, immediately confiscated the paper. According to Head, a panel of experts subsequently spent "months and several hundreds of pounds of good English money" on trying to unravel the meaning of the mysterious set of numerals.

Centuries passed, and the figures remained undecipherable, one day coming to the attention of recent immigrant John Jacob Astor (the first) or someone in league with him who took a close look at the numbers and interpreted them as latitude and longitude. The "4410" was 44 degrees, 10 minutes north latitude and the "6818" was 68 degrees, 18 minutes west longitude. These coordinates roughly correspond with the latitude and longitude of Deer Isle in Maine. This entry also demonstrates how skillful Head was at weaving a deception, by making it look just a wee bit incorrect.

Years later, according to the story, Olmsted figured out the same coordinates from the numbers and had prior knowledge that Astor or his associates had been active in the area. Having removed Kidd's treasure from a cave, Astor and friends left marks in the mud from a chest, which Olmstead had discovered.

Without pursuing all of the additional falsehoods in Head's pamphlet any further, the story of Kidd's wife and the coordinates are evidence enough of the story's impossibility. They are also a surprising oversight on Head's part, as he seemed to thrive on detail.

In fact, Kidd's wife never went to London for his trial—she remained in New York. And while latitude was used for navigation in Kidd's time, the mathematics for longitude had not yet been developed. Therefore, the scenario of Kidd in London handing his wife a note with latitude and longitude on it is patently impossible, which debunks this Kidd Deer Island treasure story.

Another story of Kidd's treasure in Maine involves Davis Island, located on the east side of the Sheepscot River where Route 1 crosses between the village of Wiscasset and the town of Edgecomb. This story was well researched by Wiscasset-area historical author Phil Di Vece, who gleaned the details from an 1859 tome written by Rufus King Sewall and a book by Wiscasset chronicler

Fanny S. Chase written in the 1930s. The information from both volumes was checked independently, and Di Vece's version, published by the *Wiscasset Newspaper* in 2015, was found to be absolutely accurate (in contrast with the writings of previously mentioned Franklin Head).

Maine was still a sparsely populated domain, and Davis Island was known as Folly Island at the time of these occurrences. One of the earliest settlers in the area was Samuel Trask, and it was his son who told Sewall the story of Captain Kidd's relationship with his father and the possibility of buried treasure on Folly Island.

However, the reader will find that while Di Vece's representation of the published facts is correct, his own keen observations leave some doubt as to how accurate young Trask's telling of the story was, and/or or Sewall's version of it.

The "legend," as Di Vece refers to it, begins when Samuel Trask was a young boy. He was captured by Native Americans in Salem, Massachusetts, and taken north into Maine. While living with the Native Americans, he was taught all of the survival skills required to exist in the woods. Later, he was sold to a Frenchman, then captured by the English and somehow joined up with Captain Kidd. During his time sailing with Kidd, Trask said he participated in burying a pot of gold coins on the east side of Davis/Folly Island. In later years, he returned to the area and built a log cabin on the Heights, located on the east side of the Sheepscot River. There is no indication he ever recovered the buried treasure or even tried to. Trask raised a family and perhaps lived a very long life. He claimed to have celebrated his 118th birthday prior to his death in 1789.

However, the thorough research of Di Vece located a genealogical source that placed Trask's birth date at 1703 in Salem, making it more likely that he was actually about eighty-six years old when he passed. Di Vece's information on Trask's date of birth provides another revelation: Kidd was executed in 1701, making it impossible for him to have ever spent time with Trask.

Perhaps, like the story of his 118th birthday, Trask was given to telling a tall tale on occasion, and one of these may have been the buried treasure on Davis Island. As so often occurs with tales of treasure, the questionable facts in the story of Kidd's pot of gold coins hasn't deterred eager treasure hunters. According to Di Vece, there have been people digging in the area and even dragging the Sheepscot River bottom, seeking the lost fortune. (Would-be seekers should be advised that Davis Island is private property.)

Another story of Captain Kidd on the Maine Coast is told by Charlotte Beath Brown in her 1926 book *In Old Boothbay: The Brick House and Other*

Stories. In her introduction, Brown noted the stories in her book were based on, "some local tradition or historical fact," so it's not entirely clear which of these is the source for her chapter "The Black Flag in Oven's Mouth." (The common modern usage is Ovens Mouth, without the apostrophe.)

Ovens Mouth is a narrow natural channel occurring in the Back River of Boothbay, which is a tidal river. During the change of tides, the water forced through these narrows becomes quite turbulent. These tidal changes affect the activities of everyone in the area, which is why, on a date not specified by Brown, a young girl named Faith, whose family lived at a nearby farm, was instructed by her father to check tidal conditions for fishing so he could continue working on home repairs.

As she neared the shore, Faith spotted a strange ship at anchor and a group of men, apparently sailors from the ship, who were hard at work cutting wood. Their leader kept a watchful eye over them, and she noted that they addressed him as "William Kidd." Naturally cautious, Faith kept out of sight, eyeing them suspiciously until she quietly turned and retreated back to the family cabin.

Of course, Faith had no idea of who William Kidd was, so when she described the men to her father, she was surprised when her father reacted in a panic at the mention of the name.

"Kidd here!" her father cried hoarsely. "I am undone! My fate has pursued me; if William Kidd is here, I am a lost man. Kidd will never spare the man who would have betrayed him."

The tale goes on to describe how Faith's father, a former member of Kidd's crew who somehow went astray of the pirate captain, returned to the shoreline location in the night hours and surreptitiously observed Kidd and his crew burying a chest loaded with gold coins and precious gems. He is quietly followed at some distance by Faith, who provides "witness testimony" to support the story.

Attempting to conceal himself in the dark woods, Faith's father (who is never named except for his pirate moniker "Long Jack") waited and watched, hoping for the pirate crew to finish their work and leave so he could keep the treasure for himself. However, a thunderstorm suddenly rolled in, and a flash of lighting revealed Long Jack's presence to Capt. Kidd. The two men, locked in combat, rolled down toward the riverbank as the storm began in earnest, bringing gusty winds, heavy rainfall and high waves to the area. Suddenly, a huge surge of wind-driven water came rolling up through Ovens Mouth, enveloped the shoreline and swept both men into deep, turbulent, water and out of sight.

Pirates and Lost Treasure of Coastal Maine

When the skies had cleared next morning, and young Faith returned to the battered shoreline of Back River, there was no sign of the treasure chest or the pirate ship. There was also no sign of Faith's father, who, according to the tale, "The Oven's Mouth had opened to receive him, there to remain until the sea gives up its dead."

According to the tale, "subsequent events" prove that Kidd survived, but "not long after this he was captured and taken to England where his execution took place."

The final disposition of the treasure chest was not so clearly described in the story. "Perhaps the mighty arms of the storm had dragged it out and buried it beneath the waves, or had cast it down in the place designed for it and buried the earth over it so firmly that never again would it be raised by human hands," the tale speculated, adding, "visitors to that part of Boothbay may still be shown an oddly shaped stone which marks the spot where Kidd's treasure is said to be buried."

The timing of this story, just prior to Kidd's well-documented arrival in New York and arrest in Boston, certainly makes it unlikely that the pirates described in this tale included Kidd, who was well known to be traveling from the south aboard a merchant sloop, not a pirate ship. Of course, "some local tradition or historical fact" (as Brown described her sources) may have included a visit to Ovens Mouth from pirates or sea rovers other than Kidd, spawning a basis for the tale.

The "oddly shaped stone" mentioned by Brown adds an enticing end to the tale; marking Kidd's buried hoard, it may still be resting along the shoreline at Ovens Mouth. For those who would like to seek this stone, Ovens Mouth is now a preserve maintained by the Boothbay Region Land Trust and open to the public with a number of excellent hiking trails, several of which skirt the shoreline. Perhaps an intrepid visitor might pass over a fortune in gold and jewels buried by a sudden storm and the passage of time, marked only by an "oddly shaped stone."

5

PIRATE TREASURE IN MACHIAS

During the so-called Golden Age of Piracy from the late 1600s to the early 1700s, several well-known pirate enclaves were established, including one in Maine. With a preponderance of pirates, and their loot, these locations thrived—at least for a while.

On the island of Île Sainte-Marie (now known, for reasons unexplained, as Nosy Boraha) off the northeast coast of Madagascar, a former pirate–turned–entrepreneur named Adam Baldridge, fleeing a murder charge in Jamaica, established a supply station and "rest stop" for pirates preying on ships plying the Indian Ocean. Île Sainte-Marie wasn't defended by any major country, so it was an easy place for the pirates to settle in.

The island was conveniently located for ships on the "Pirate Round," which brought crews from Europe and the Americas around the Cape of Good Hope near the southern tip of Africa and up the East African coast. Depleted from the long voyage, the ships and their crews would put into Île Sainte-Marie, where there was plenty of rum for the pirate crews and whatever marine supplies Baldridge could obtain for the captains.

Once restocked and rested from their shore leave, the buccaneers would set a northerly course and lie in wait for ships bringing trade goods from India and southeast Asia, as well as Muslims on pilgrimage to Mecca. (It's important to note that in the absence of credit cards and traveler's cheques, pilgrims and other travelers were in the practice of carrying vast amounts of valuables to cover their expenses.)

Pirates and Lost Treasure of Coastal Maine

Much like today's pirates based in Somalia, these buccaneers would take advantage of the restrictive passage at the Gulf of Aden to make their hunting easy and profitable.

Baldridge's business venture as a pirate refuge began in 1685 and continued to be successful before ending in 1697, when the indigenous population rose up against him for selling off some of their members as slaves. The way station continued under Edward Welsh, followed by John Pro, but they were never quite as successful as Baldridge, and the enclave was abandoned in 1719 upon Pro's death.

The island continues to be a popular tourist destination, where visitors can stroll through a graveyard filled with weather-beaten headstones marking pirate graves.

In the Caribbean, pirates established an enclave in 1703 at present-day Nassau, which had been rendered vulnerable by Spanish attacks and mostly abandoned by English settlers, who had either left the island or fled inland. By 1713, there were over one thousand pirates active at the location, coming and going as they raided shipping along the American southeastern seaboard and into the eastern Caribbean. The area was frequented by some of the best-known pirates of the Caribbean—Blackbeard, Calico Jack Rackham and Stede Bonnet—as well as little-known, but more successful captains such as Benjamin Hornigold (also known as Thornigold), who, for a short while, became the de facto ruler of the buccaneer roost.

All the pirate fun ended in 1718, when an English force under Woodes Rogers invaded the enclave and shut down piracy, including an offer of amnesty for pirates who would quit the "sweet trade." The deal effectively ended the pirate colony.

According to a variety of historical and modern sources, the area of Machias Bay and into the Machias River, located on the northern coast of Maine, was also targeted for a pirate settlement.

In his highly regarded book *The Republic of Pirates*, author Colin Woodard notes that the War of Spanish Succession (1701–1714), which drew English resources away from the American settlements, had left the coast of Maine in much the same condition as the Bahamas. "The Indians and their French allies had burned most of the English settlements, leaving hundreds of miles of coastline uninhabited, including countless anchorages where an entire fleet of ships could refit unobserved by European eyes. Most important, the shores were covered in forests, with so many great pines that "the Royal Navy itself relied on the region to supply its warships with pitch, lumber and masts," Woodard wrote.

Pirates and Lost Treasure of Coastal Maine

Maine also provided the pirates with an excellent summertime base, free of tropical heat and dangerous hurricanes but still close enough to American ports in the south and French ports in modern-day Canada to the north to allow for easy commerce raiding. When winter settled in, migrating pirates could continue to take ships as they traveled south to the Caribbean. Likewise, in the spring, they could cruise north from the Caribbean, plundering the numerous vessels that were actively trading with the colonies after a long winter with little or no shipping.

The geography of Machias was also well suited to their needs, with a large bay facing the Atlantic Ocean, a navigable river and a narrows bordered on both sides by high ground, making for an effective land-based defense against any intruding vessel.

Therefore, it comes as no surprise that there were a number of pirates and privateers active in the area and that there are still locations in the Machias area rumored to hold hidden troves of treasure.

The best known of these pirates is Black Sam Bellamy, whose travels, as documented by noted pirate historian Ken Kinkor, are described in chapter 7 of this book. According to Kinkor and his detailed research, Bellamy never made it to Machias, instead going down with his ship the *Whydah* (pronounced "wid-ah," derived from the name of a slave port on the West African coast) and about four tons of treasure during a storm off Wellfleet, Massachusetts, in April 1717.

However, there are some modern-day Machias locals who disagree with Kinkor's research, believing instead that Bellamy had already visited Machias and concealed most of his treasure there before heading south to Wellfleet to pick up settlers for his pirate enclave, including his love interest Mary Hallett. This was all described in *A General History of the Pyrates*, a somewhat controversial tome. According to this version, the *Whydah* was lost before Bellamy could complete this mission and return, leaving his treasure behind in Machias, according to the locals.

Multiple sources report that there are at least six known locations in the Machias area where treasure may be hidden. Moreover, there was another well-known pirate several experts believe frequented the area, reportedly leaving a treasure cache and fort, but whose association with Machias has been lost to history, save for a few enticing clues. That pirate was Olivier Levasseur, also known as Olivier La Buse, Louis Labous, La Bouse, La Bouche and La Buze. La Buze "The Buzzard" and La Bouche "The Mouth" were somehow references to how Levasseur attacked his enemies.

[cryptogram image]

A cryptogram allegedly created by the pirate Olivier Levasseur that is said to lead to hidden treasure, perhaps in Machais, for anyone who can decode it. It should be noted that some researchers believe this cryptogram to be a hoax. *Bibliotheque Nationale (France)*.

The theory behind Levasseur's connection with Machias was first put forward by Ken Kinkor, the Black Sam Bellamy researcher previously mentioned, during a 2009 interview conducted by this author. Kinkor believed that the writer or writers of *A General History of the Pyrates*, which describes Bellamy's presence in Machias, might have mistaken Levasseur for Bellamy.

Kinkor's reasoning was set forth in a 2012 article in the *Portland Press Herald* written by the aforementioned Colin Woodard. Woodard posited:

Pirates and Lost Treasure of Coastal Maine

What if someone else did the deeds The General History *ascribed to Bellamy?...One thing I learned about* General History *is that its author or authors only rarely invented passages, but regularly confused timing, events, and particularly the identities of individual pirates, especially when several gangs were operating in the same area with similarly sized vessels. I suspect that's exactly what happened in the Machias-and-Newfoundland passage, which is remarkably fine-grained and detailed to have not been based on actual events, even if they were garbled.*

La Buse and Bellamy were longtime acquaintances, at least in "pirate time." They were both part of a buccaneer fleet under pirate leaders Benjamin Hornigold (also known as Thornigold) and Henry Jennings, circa 1716 cruising the Caribbean in search of prey. This fleet was a virtual who's who of pirates at the time, known as "The Flying Gang," that ultimately included Edward Teach (also known as Blackbeard), Richard Noland, Paulsgrave Williams, William Howard, Charles Vane, Stede Bonnet and Edward England.

When the Flying Gang split up about a year later, Levasseur fell in with Bellamy for a short time, who had also formed an alliance with Paulsgrave Williams (a friend of Bellamy's from his original pirate days) and Richard Nolan. (More about Bellamy, his cohorts and their connection with Maine in another chapter.)

According to English records located by Woodard, Levasseur was sighted in July 1717 on an easterly course crossing the coast of Maine. (It should be noted here that due to the shape of the Maine coastline, a generally easterly course, with a bit of northerly drift, would put the ship on a course right along the Maine shore.)

During that same period, according to Woodard's research, Levasseur told the captain of a sloop he captured in Virginia that he was on his way to New England, where he would meet a consort ship. The consort may have been Bellamy's *Whydah*, Woodard wrote. Later, a British naval officer in Boston described a pirate ship matching Levasseur's vessel that "plundered several ships and vessels" in the New England area and asserted that it was the only pirate ship active in the area for several weeks.

According to pirate researcher Laura Nelson, the *Boston Newsletter* attributed a pirate attack on the ship *Dispatch* to Levasseur in July 1717. The action took place offshore of Midcoast Maine in the vicinity of Damariscove, Monhegan and Matinicus Islands, with Levasseur in command of a 250-ton ship with twenty guns and a crew of two hundred.

Pirates and Lost Treasure of Coastal Maine

French archival documents located by Woodard detailed a pirate attack on the Grand Banks fishing fleet during this same period. All of these well-referenced reports would indicate that Levasseur was indeed active in the Maine area on a coastwise course that would have brought him close to Machias Bay and perhaps into the river.

After these sightings, Levasseur wasn't seen for another ten months, when he was reported off the east coast of South America, according to Woodard. (There is a report that Levasseur was seen in the Bahamas between September and December 1717, but this could not be corroborated.)

Those months of absence would have given Levasseur plenty of time to put into Machias during the summer season—perhaps he constructed a stockade for protection from Native Americans and any European raiders and even left a treasure cache to set aside for a future return.

However, during the 2009 interview, Kinkor's highly qualified speculation regarding pirate activity in Machias didn't end there. He also speculated that a Dutch privateer predating Levasseur might have left loot and structures behind.

Another cryptogram allegedly created by the pirate Olivier Levasseur that is said to lead to hidden treasure. Some researchers believe this cryptogram may also be a hoax. *Bibliotheque Nationale (France).*

Pirates and Lost Treasure of Coastal Maine

In a story somewhat lost to history, Machias and a large section of the northern Maine coast under French control was conquered in 1674 during the Franco-Dutch War by Dutch privateer Captain Jurriaen Aemoutsz, commanding the frigate *Flying Horse*. Two lightly defended French forts were quickly overrun by the 110 fighters under Aemoutsz's command; one of them was the capital of Acadia at the time, Fort Pentagouet, the site of present-day Castine in Maine, the oldest permanent settlement in New England. The area was given the name New Holland, and steps were taken to consolidate the takeover, including the establishment of trade by a Massachusetts man named John Rhoades (sometimes known as Rhodes), who the Dutch licensed for the task. The Dutch also appointed a governor of New Holland, Cornelis van Steenwijk, who was given responsibility for the coasts and countries of Nova Scotia and Acadia, although he remained comfortably ensconced in New York.

Rhoades traveled to the area and began trading with the Native American Wabanakis, as well as harassing English shipping. It is unclear if Rhoades built any structures or left any caches, but Kinkor noted that the opportunity was certainly there.

In the meantime, Captain Aemoutsz loaded up anything he could find of value, including cannon from the forts, then sailed to Boston and sold it all off before continuing south to new adventures in Curacao.

The Dutch never had a chance to reinforce New Holland with regular troops to consolidate the capture of their territory, and after the withdrawal of Captain Aemoutsz and his privateers, there were no defenders. The French recaptured both forts in 1676, and the Treaty of Nijmegen ended the Franco-Dutch War in 1678.

Other lesser-known pirates also visited the area, although their activities were not as well referenced as those of Levasseur or the Dutch privateers.

A pirate captain named Harry Thompson is said to have left a lifetime worth of plunder buried near his homestead on the western side of the entrance to Machias Bay, according to W.C. Jameson in his book *Buried Treasures of the Atlantic Coast*. Thompson's treasure hoard is reportedly located in an area known as Starboard, so named because, for ships leaving the bay, this shoreline would have been on the starboard (right) side of the vessel. In addition to the neighborhood, there are an island and a creek that share the name.

Jameson doesn't mention any dates but describes Thompson as a commerce raider plying the Atlantic from New England to Europe and Africa, taking at least twenty-four ships during an eleven-year pirating

Pirates and Lost Treasure of Coastal Maine

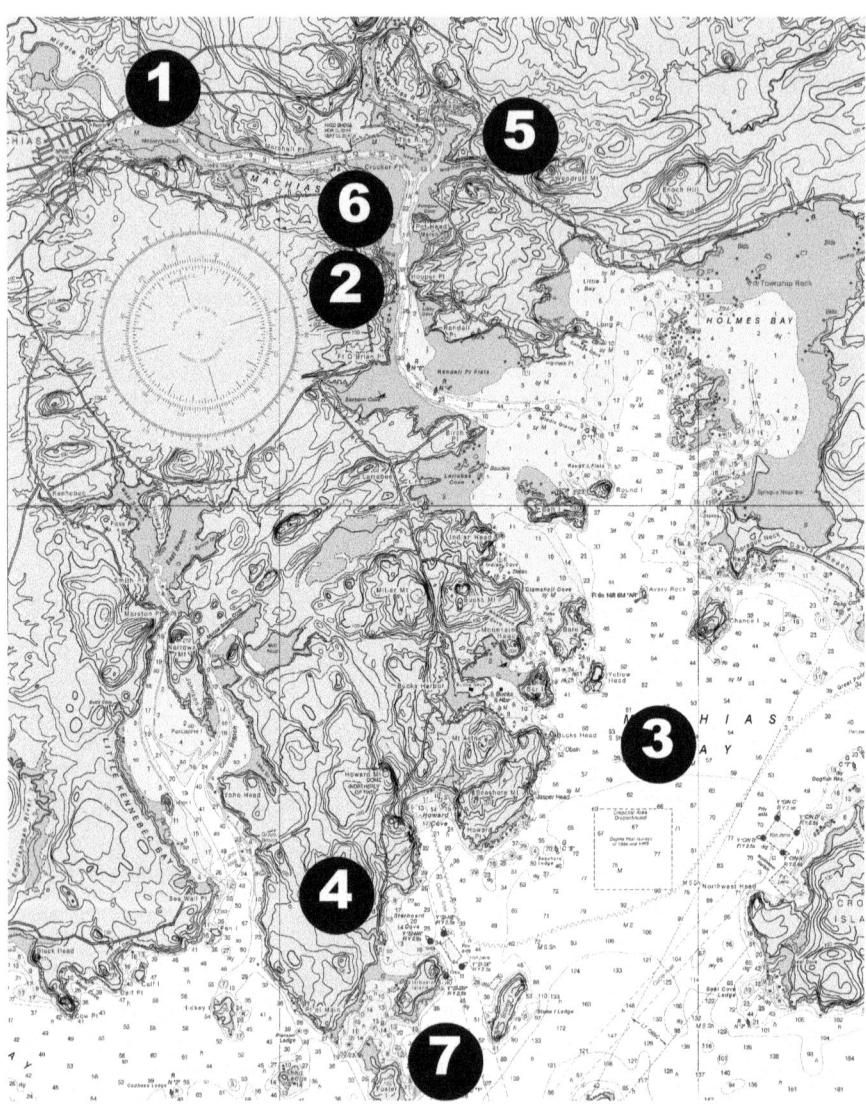

A map of the Machias area in Maine with locations marked that may have experienced pirate activity described in this chapter: 1) the present-day town of Machias; 2) the easily defended narrows on the Machias River; 3) Machias Bay; 4) Starboard Cove and Starboard Island, so named because they are on the starboard side of ships exiting Machias Bay; 5) Simpson Island, offshore of Shipyard Cove; 6) Renshaw Point; 7) Brother Island. *United States Geological Survey.*

career. He was joined in this effort by a buccaneer known only as "Starbird"; however, there are some who speculate that "Starbird" may just be a name born out of confusion with the Starboard region.

Thompson is said to have returned regularly to his homestead to make treasure deposits in his secret stash, all while maintaining a low profile both locally and at sea in order to avoid the authorities. While on shore in Machias he preserved his image as that of a frugal seafarer, and the other residents of Machias never suspected him.

When Thompson decided to leave the sweet trade of piracy, he established a farm on the site. Thompson shared out the treasure with Starbird, who is said to have quietly loaded a seafaring vessel and sailed off, never to be heard from again. Thompson settled into the quiet life of a Maine farmer, raising a family and occasionally visiting his stash to collect a small amount of coinage. He never revealed his secret location or anything about his piratical past, not even to his family. Yet somewhere near his idyllic farm, nestled in the woods that grow right up to the shoreline, eleven years of buccaneer booty lay hidden underground.

Age began to creep up on Thompson, and he knew someday his children would have to inherit the treasure, but he didn't want to reveal the location outright. He began to take solitary walks in the woods, making cryptic marks on stones and trees that he hoped in the future would lead his offspring to the hoard. He then sat down with a piece of parchment, quill and ink and began drawing out a map of his property and the buildings, without revealing the exact location of his plunder. He passed away with his secret still known only to him, but hopeful the clues he left behind would lead his family to the hidden riches.

Years after Thompson's death, his son Willis, having grown to manhood, located the map along with a note describing a treasure stash on the property. Willis began exploring the woods looking for drawings on rocks and trees. At one point, he is said to have constructed a special plow with an extended blade that he used to till fields in the area, hoping that the deep-running blade would strike an underground object—perhaps the treasure-trove. Despite his efforts, Willis never found what could have been his inheritance, estimated to be millions of dollars' worth of gold, silver and jewels, still apparently lying underground in the vicinity of Starboard Creek.

Simpson Island is another Machias area where pirate treasure may have been concealed. A heavily forested bit of land located in the East Machias River near Shipyard Cove, Simpson Island is not too far from where US Route 1 passes through Machias. Somewhere on the riverbanks surrounding

A view of the Machias River from the north bank near the town of Machias. *Author photo.*

this island there is an unconfirmed report that treasure hunters unearthed a kettle filled with hidden riches in the 1960s.

Renshaw Point is located just downriver from Simpson Island on the west side of the Machias River. It is thought to be an area where pirates may have built a fort and perhaps a treasure cache. It is located just north of a narrows in the Machias River, with Machiasport on the west bank and Hooper Point on the east bank. This narrows would have presented an excellent defensive position, with firing positions on either bank denying access to any intruders. Some Machias locals believe that Black Sam Bellamy may have built a treasure vault in this area that is still filled with plunder when Bellamy and his ship failed to return to Machias after being lost to a storm in Massachusetts.

Finally, a pair of pirate brothers named Flynn are rumored to have used Brothers Island, located some distance due south of Starboard Island, as a hiding place for their ill-gotten gains. However, very little corroboration could be established for this tale.

Pirates and Lost Treasure of Coastal Maine

For those who dream of one day finding a pirate treasure, the Machias area has plenty to offer: a fairly well-established history of pirates and privateers, and plenty of not so well-established tales and rumors. Perhaps there is a trove of pirate plunder waiting to be unearthed, or perhaps the lucky treasure hunter may turn up valuables of a different kind, such as historic artifacts that clarify the colorful history in this section of the Maine coastline.

6

BARTHOLOMEW ROBERTS'S TREASURE IN PHIPPSBURG

In perhaps what may be the best historical example of how the rocky coast of Maine figured into the Golden Age of Piracy is a tale of epic seafaring adventure and violent confrontation that culminated in the early 1900s with the discovery of buried treasure alongside the Kennebec River.

According to some authors, while a fortune in treasure was discovered in a buried chest at the riverside location, the fortune seekers missed another two chests that may still be concealing a pirate's long-lost hoard. The original text that describes the secret location is included in this chapter, but it is highly likely that the geography has changed substantially, perhaps leaving the trove of priceless valuables hidden forevermore—or awaiting accidental discovery by some lucky soul.

Multiple published sources have reported that the treasure included many gold coins and a pearl necklace, but the centerpiece of the find was a large gold cross, studded with gems. This cross was said to be worn in battle by the highly religious pirate captain Bartholomew Roberts, known after his death as "Black Bart." (It is likely no one would dare refer to him by his nickname during his lifetime out of concern for their own personal safety. "Black" referred to his long, black hair.)

Roberts was active in piracy between 1719 and 1722, raiding locations north to Nova Scotia and south to the west coast of Africa. This route could have certainly included stops on the coast of Maine or any number of islands offshore of Maine.

Roberts was a colorful and fiercely independent individual whose lifetime was well documented, and he is thus a compelling example of how pirates, and their treasure, were all a part of Maine history.

His name at birth, in the Welsh village of Casnewydd-Bach, circa 1682, was John Roberts, according to Lisa Yount in her 2002 book *Pirates*. At some point, he changed his first name. There is speculation that he may have decided to fashion his own identity around that of a popular pirate at the time, Bartholomew Sharp.

Not much was recorded about his early life. There is speculation he went to sea in his early teens, with the first seafaring record of him in 1718 as a mate on a Barbados sloop, a single-masted sailboat that would have been used for inter-island commerce in the Caribbean.

In 1719, he is recorded by some sources as a mate on the slave ship *Princess* out of London and by other sources as the ship's master. The most likely scenario, based on combined sources, was that he was a navigator on the *Princess*, which would have afforded him the rank of second or third officer.

Bartholomew Roberts shown in an engraving depicting him at Whydah on the West African coastline, with his two ships *Royal Fortune* (right) and *Ranger* (center) under sail with pirate flags aloft. The illustrator may have exaggerated the size and armament of the vessels. *Engraving by Benjamin Cole, public domain.*

Pirates and Lost Treasure of Coastal Maine

The *Princess* sailed out of the Thames in London, turning south and off to the west coast of Africa ready to pay for and pick up its tragic cargo of human chattel, putting into port at Annamboa in present-day Ghana. On board would have been enough coinage and valuables to pay for the cargo of slaves awaiting delivery to the plantations of the Caribbean.

So it was no surprise that a pirate crew lurking in the vicinity of Annamboa took a special interest in the *Princess* and its treasure hoard. The pirates, under Captain Howell Davis, attacked with two ships, both barks—rigged for sail, each with two decks of guns. These ships were the *Royal Rover* and the *Royal James*, both quickly overpowering the hapless crew of the *Princess*. Roberts was forced to join the pirate crew against his will so they could take advantage of his skills as a navigator, which was common for skilled trades like carpenters, surgeons and, notably, musicians.

Despite the fact that Roberts was essentially a prisoner, he developed a relationship with the pirate captain Davis, who turned out to be a fellow Welshman. The captain would ask for, and honor, Roberts's opinions. Sometimes they would speak to each other in Welsh so crewmembers couldn't understand them.

Apparently, one thing led to another, and Roberts finally decided to join the buccaneer crew in the sweet trade, as piracy was then known—at least to pirates.

Roberts's transformation from an honest sailor to a pirate was not an unusual transition at the time. A sailor lived a dangerous life in miserable conditions for low wages. The pirate life was far cry from that of the common sailor. Generally, pirates shared out their captured plunder in amounts previously agreed to that were nearly equal in portion. For example, a crew member might get a full share, while a captain was awarded a share and half. Depending on how lucrative the captures were, a pirate crew member could end a voyage either set for life—or at least for several months of very good times.

Many pirate crews, including the buccaneers under Captain Davis, were able to vote their leadership in or out, in peaceful elections, with every person getting a full vote regardless of rank. Such voting, with each person having a full say in a crew made up of nationalities from around the world, was unheard of on shore in those times. (More about this is discussed in chapter 2.)

For captured sailors, or even those in port between ships, an invitation to piracy might well seem like a step up in status, even though a hangman's noose might be their only retirement option.

Pirates and Lost Treasure of Coastal Maine

Roberts was later quoted in *A General History of the Pyrates*:

> *In an honest service there is thin commons, low wages, and hard labour. In this* [piracy], *plenty and satiety, pleasure and ease, liberty and power; and who would not balance* [the] *creditor on this side, when the hazard that is run for it, at worst is only a sour look or two at choking?* [From hanging.] *No, a merry life and a short one shall be my motto.*

The fact that pirate crews elected their captains was to become an important factor for Roberts, as a fateful destiny awaited the pirate ship and its crew.

After securing their captured treasure from *Princess*, the pirates prepared to raise sails and head out on the search for more profit and prizes. However, it soon became apparent that damage caused by wood-eating worms infesting the hull of *Royal James* was making the ship unsafe. Its cargo and crew were crowded onto the *Royal Rover*, and the *Royal James* was scuttled.

Bearing east by south into the Gulf of Guinea, likely keeping within sight of the shoreline, the pirates aboard *Royal Rover* set their course to the island of Principe, a Portuguese colony situated on fifty-three square miles of ancient volcano several hundred miles due west of the African mainland. The colonists on the island were quite well-to-do, having established sugar and cocoa plantations there with slave labor from the mainland.

The island's harbor at Santo Antonio was protected by an infantry company fortified by the majestic Fortaleza de Santo Antonio de Ponta with pieces of heavy bronze artillery, enough to make any seaborne invaders a wee bit nervous.

But Captain Davis had a plan that would bring his ship and crew right under those guns and allow them to make off with a considerable sum of treasure, hopefully without a shot being fired by either side.

In past adventures, Captain Davis had been successful in using playacting and subterfuge to gain advantage over his intended targets, twice resulting in bloodless victories for the conniving captain.

In one instance, he portrayed himself as a privateer pirate hunter to the English commander of a fort in Gambia operated by the Royal Africa Company for slaving operations. At a dinner celebration to welcome him, Captain Davis, the guest of honor, and his pirate crew instead captured the English commander and held him for ransom, demanding £2,000 in gold. Once paid, the pirates left the commander and other inhabitants unharmed and sailed merrily off into the south Atlantic, with £2,000 now in their cargo hold.

On another occasion, in order to intimidate a well-armed but smaller French merchant vessel, Captain Davis ran up a black flag of no mercy while aboard a larger and very intimidating—but lightly armed—ship he had just captured. The French merchant crew quickly surrendered.

Now Captain Davis hatched a new plan and briefed his crew. They would call on Santo Antonio, using the guise of a privateer pirate hunter once again. As soon as good relations were established with the Portuguese governor, said governor would be invited aboard the *Royal Rover* for a grand party (sometimes called a "bacchanal" in the pirate vernacular of the time).

Once aboard, and perhaps after a few fermented beverages to soften the blow, the governor would be taken prisoner and a ransom demanded. While not recorded, the plan would have likely included an escape strategy calling for the governor to remain aboard the pirate ship once the ransom was paid, offering the pirates a chance to sail out of range from the fort's cannon before allowing the governor to board some small boat to row his way back to Principe.

The *Royal Rover* dropped anchor in the port of Santo Antonio in late June 1719, and Captain Davis began work to put his plan into play. However, a prisoner aboard the pirate ship had overheard crewmembers discussing Captain Davis's nefarious plot and decided to make a bid for freedom, along with the chance for a handsome reward from the Portuguese. Under the cover of darkness that night, the prisoner quietly slipped over the side of ship and swam ashore, warning local authorities of the impending capture of the governor.

The next morning, June 19, 1719, the Portuguese on Principe decided to give Captain Davis a taste of his own medicine.

They extended an invitation to the captain and his crew to come ashore for a welcoming reception. Captain Davis, apparently unaware that the escaped prisoner had revealed his plot, eagerly accepted the offer of local wine and headed to shore with a few members of his crew. Upon landing, he was welcomed not only by some seemingly friendly local officials but also by a squad of soldiers from the fort who lay in wait for him farther along the path. It must have taken only a few seconds for the soldiers to cut loose with a hail of musketry, likely followed by close work with short swords, to end the buccaneering careers of Captain Howell Davis and all of the crewmembers accompanying him.

Back on board the *Royal Rover*, the astonished pirates on deck, including Roberts, must have heard the gunfire and quickly realized the plan had gone astray. They must have nervously eyed the bronze artillery pieces lined up in the fort and realized their ship was now a big fish in a very small pond. Probably cutting the cable to their anchor, then laying on sail as fast as they could, the pirates must have breathed a collective sigh of relief as they left Principe and the deadly shore guns in their wake.

Back on the island of Principe, the residents must have celebrated as they watched the *Royal Rover*'s sails disappear over the horizon. Perhaps some wine bottles were opened, and a party ensued, filled with merriment and laughter. Little did the Principeans know who would have the last laugh.

Now safely out to sea, the pirate crew had another challenge. Who would be their next captain?

Perhaps surprisingly for a new member of the crew, Roberts was one of several pirates to be nominated for the captain's position. Various sources attribute the crew's nomination of Roberts to consideration of his skill as a navigator as well as his charismatic personality.

According to *A General History of the Pyrates*, one of the crew members made the following speech on Roberts's behalf:

> *It is my advice, while we are sober, to pitch upon a man of courage, and skilled in navigation, one who, by his prudence and bravery, seems best able to defend this commonwealth, and ward us from the dangers and tempests of an unstable element, and the fatal consequences of anarchy; and such a one I take Roberts to be: A fellow in all respects worthy of your esteem and favor.*

Roberts won the election easily, and according to *A General History of the Pyrates*, he gave this acceptance speech: "Since I have dipped my hands in muddy water and must be a pirate, it is better being a commander than a private man."

The first order of business for the new captain was to avenge the death of his friend Captain Davis, and for that purpose. Roberts gathered his crew and plotted a devastating return to Principe.

Descriptions of the assault on Principe vary, but most begin with the *Royal Rover* slipping into the port under cover of early morning darkness, sending a party of about thirty well-armed buccaneers ashore and then opening fire on the fort with the ship's guns. The cannonade sent the Portuguese soldiers scrambling from their fortress and into the nearby jungle, while residents in the town must have been jolted from their slumber.

The landing party swarmed into the fort and pushed the cannon deployed there off the parapets and into the sea; then, the story seems to vary. In one version, the invaders enter the town and kill off most of the male population, laying the area to waste and making off with anything of value. In another version, Roberts warns the pirates that the infantrymen in the jungle still presented a threat and withdrew the shore party without leaving much damage. In either case, Roberts's first foray was judged a success, and now the pirates turned their attention to new prey.

Captain Bartholomew Roberts became the most successful pirate of the era, taking over four hundred ships during his nearly three-year career. He was well known for his stylish dress in battle, sporting a crimson waistcoat and breeches and a red feather in a large hat, grasping an elegant sword and carrying two pairs of pistols likely hung around his neck and tied off, each equally, to a silken ribbon for easy access. Such a pistol arrangement would have been the fast-draw rig of the time It would allow the user to grasp a weapon and discharge it, then quickly drop it with the ribbon still retaining it, so the user could grab another pistol and fire it. Roberts's rig, with two pairs of pistols, would allow him to quickly fire four times without having to reload any of the single-shot weapons at his immediate disposal.

Perhaps most noteworthy in Roberts's attire was the large gold cross, described earlier, studded with jewels that hung from a heavy necklace. This may have reflected his strong religious beliefs, the same beliefs that caused him to hold Sunday services and disallow alcohol and gambling aboard his ship.

One source describes the cross as plunder originally captured from the Portuguese merchant ship *Sagrada Familia* in the early part of Roberts's career. Part of the rich haul from the captured ship was a fortune in gold as well as trade goods, including tobacco and skins. The bejeweled religious icon was said to be part of a collection designed for the king of Portugal. The gold cross was now to follow a path with many twists and turns—a journey that, some say, would end in Maine.

The crew of *Royal Rover* laid on sail from the southeastern Atlantic and headed west by north, seeking plunder in Brazil and then on to the Caribbean from July 1719 to May 1720. During this period, Roberts boarded a captured sloop to chase down a large brigantine, leaving one of his crew, Walter Kennedy, in command of the *Royal Rover* and a small detachment of buccaneers to man the vessel.

While Roberts was chasing down the brigantine, the untrustworthy Kennedy made off with the *Royal Rover* to start his own career as a pirate captain, leaving Roberts and his remaining crew behind. On learning of the *Royal Rover*'s loss, Roberts and his cohorts simply christened their sloop the *Fortune* and continued north, looking for plunder.

Roberts was to suffer his first tactical defeat in February 1720, trapped in a cannon battle with a Barbadian/English warship of twenty guns that was disguised as a Barbadian merchant vessel.

The battle lasted several hours, and the *Fortune* sustained heavy damage and casualties before breaking off. Roberts used the faster sloop design of the *Fortune* to outrun the Barbadian.

The pirate captain took his losses in stride, repairing his ship in Bonaire, but decided to seek safer waters, especially as the hot Caribbean summer and hurricane season began to settle in. He set his sights on Newfoundland and French shipping there. His northerly course certainly must have taken him along the American East Coast and up past Maine, where he would have found many sheltered coves in which to stop over. The islands of Monhegan and Damariscove, lying just offshore Midcoast Maine, were popular layovers for coastwise sailors.

Roberts wasted no time in making his presence known after arriving in Newfoundland, utilizing a bold new tactic that may be compared with the modern military term "shock and awe." On June 21, 1720, clad in his battle regalia and wearing the golden cross, he loaded his cannon at sea with shot but no ball, and then sailed right into the narrow harbor entrance at Trepassey, while his musicians filled the quiet anchorage with the sound of trumpets and drums. Without warning, he raised his black flag of piracy, ran out his guns and released a cannonade that must have echoed menacingly off the low hills on the east side of the anchorage.

Nestled in the harbor, the terrified crews of 22 merchant ships and 150 fishing boats quickly abandoned their vessels on rowboats and pulled for the safety of shore, leaving their cargos and vessels for the pirates to plunder at will. (Note: Some versions of the attack at Trepassey have Roberts immediately burning or sinking most of the anchored fleet. However, this is unlikely, as sunken ships are hard to plunder, which is why most pirates used tactics like boarding, disabling or just plain frightening crews into surrender. Nonetheless, the reader will find that Roberts's flair for destruction would soon affect the Trepassey anchorage.)

Roberts and his pirate crew were rulers of the harbor during their stay at Trepassey, taking what they wanted from vessels at anchor and, according to some reports, coming ashore to pillage what they could from the households and farms.

As Roberts scanned the captured fleet, he noticed, with interest, a large bark riding at anchor. The term *bark* (also spelled barque and not a shortened version of barkentine, a completely different type of ship) can describe the rigging and configuration of a number of ship types, sometimes including four-masted vessels. Generally speaking, bark describes a mid-sized three-masted vessel, with the fore and main masts rigged for square sails and the mizzen (back) mast rigged with a "fore and aft" sail that could align with the ship's keel in the center of the ship. This configuration made for an easy-to-sail ship that could outperform other vessels and allow a captain many options. Such a ship would have been ideal for piracy, providing a much larger gun platform than his sloop *Fortune*, so Roberts captured the bark at Trepassey, renamed it the *Good Fortune* and fitted it out with twenty-six guns.

With this new acquisition, and his sloop *Fortune*, Roberts was building a powerful flotilla.

Roberts and his crew enjoyed their stay at Trepassey into late June, at which time they lastly burned every vessel in the harbor. Under smoke-filled skies, they cheerfully raised sails and headed out to sea. They roamed coastal Canada and down through Maine, taking many more vessels with their flotilla of black-flagged ships. Sometime in the late summer of 1720, Roberts used his skills as a navigator to gain his bearings and set a southerly course for a return to the Caribbean.

By September 1720, after continuing to capture ships while on the move, Roberts's flotilla put in to the island of Carriacou, located in the Grenadine Islands north of Grenada in the southern Caribbean, where they made repairs on their vessels and renamed the *Good Fortune* in favor of *Royal Fortune*.

At this point, there is so much additional taking and renaming of ships that accuracy becomes hard to achieve. In one case, *A General History of the Pyrates* describes Roberts as taking a fifty-two-gun French warship with the governor of Martinique on board. According to the report, Roberts hung the governor from a yardarm, and the ship was promptly converted for piracy and renamed as the new *Royal Fortune*.

However, several noted historians describe this narrative in *A General History of the Pyrates* as a complete embellishment. So, for accuracy, and the reader's convenience, we'll forego trying to follow the ships that Roberts continued to take as he headed across the South Atlantic on what becomes a fateful course for West Africa.

Roberts raided through the Cape Verde islands, then turned south, following the African coastline to Sierra Leone, where he captured and converted to pirate use two French warships. Here, he was warned by an old pirate on shore that two English warships, the HMS *Swallow* and the HMS *Weymouth*, were active in the area.

He continued raiding down the coastline, finally arriving at the mouth of the Calabar River (then known as Callebar) in present-day Nigeria about late January 1722. He was commanding a flotilla now numbering three ships, with names that at this point can be accurately described: *Royal Fortune* (the flagship), *Ranger* and *Little Ranger*. (Note: Some sources describe the fleet as numbering only two ships, which could mean that the *Little Ranger* was small enough that perhaps, in the opinion of some, it didn't warrant the ship designation.)

Aside from the assumption that the *Royal Fortune*, as flagship, was likely the largest of the three, there are no accurate descriptions available of the ships or their configurations. Most descriptions of past ships commanded by Roberts under various names say the vessels were armed with about twenty-six guns. One report in *A General History of the Pyrates*, attributed to Royal Navy officers, has the *Royal Fortune* armed with forty guns at the time and the *Ranger* at thirty-two guns.

There is an illustration of these two vessels in the port of Whydah (or Ouidah) on the West African coast, where they are configured as barks with two-gun decks. It should be noted that it was common at the time for illustrations to be fanciful.

The Calabar River mouth is located on the northern side of an expansive bay that is somewhat restricted to the south by a large island. Accounts describe Roberts in the area of Parrot Island, which is located just inside the mouth of the river. He is also described as careening his vessels at the time, a cleaning process described earlier that allows the crew access to the hull. A detailed map from 1820 of the Calabar River shows areas of "sand dry at high tide" just upriver from Parrot Island, which was the ideal situation for careening.

The map also has soundings for and drawings of the river entrance, which is a strikingly narrow passage. There is considerable shoaling to the west of the river mouth. In order to gain entry, a vessel must locate and closely follow a precarious channel to the east side of the river mouth, with depths of about thirty feet and the width at the thinnest point less than one league (about three miles, although this definition varies). To follow the channel, a ship's captain would have to proceed slowly, using both his experience and a lead line for depth soundings, to make a heading of almost due north, before veering to starboard (right) to gain the next section of channel and not run aground. After sailing about three leagues upriver, and using landmarks such as a creek mouth and a spit of land called Fish Town in 1820, the captain would have to make a port (left) tack north by west to avoid grounding on

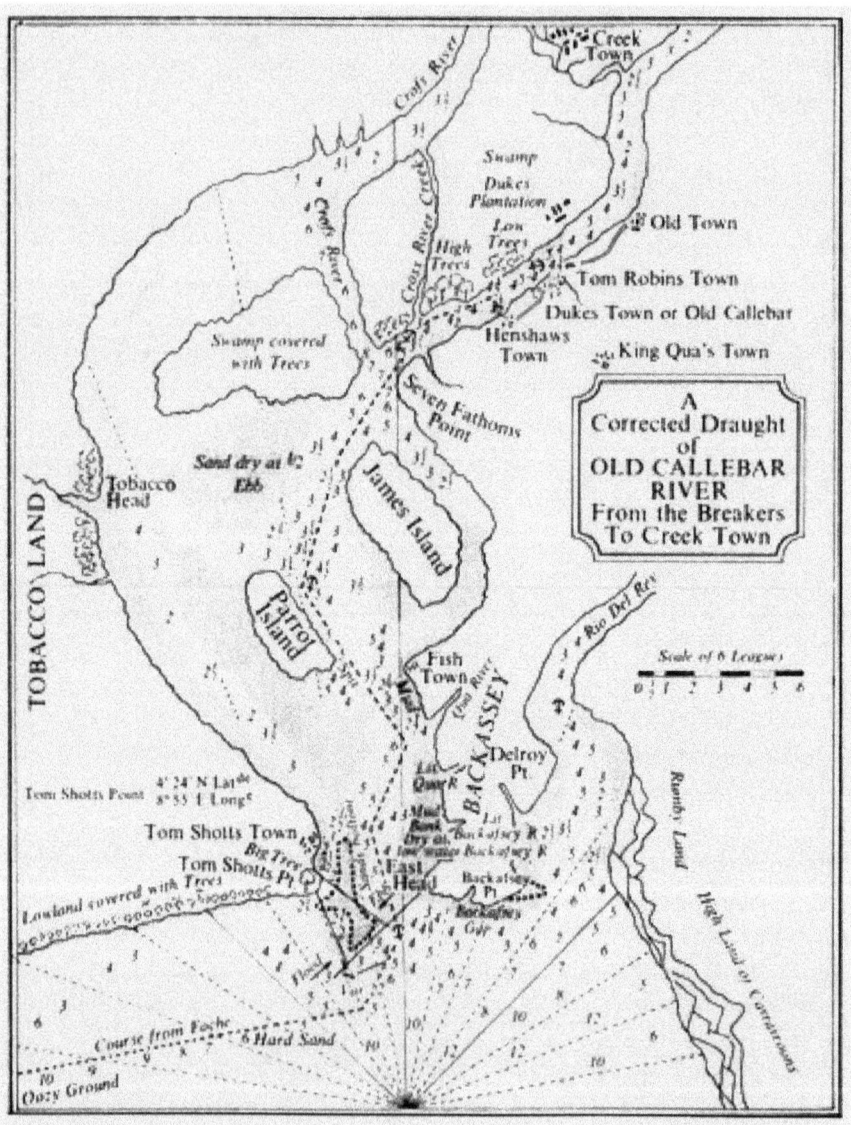

A very detailed map from 1820 of the Calabar River area (then known as Callebar). The action between the HMS *Swallow* and Roberts's *Royal Fortune* was likely fought in the channel just southeast of Parrot Island. *Public domain.*

nearby shoals before gaining a shallow anchorage of about twenty-four feet in depth that lies between Parrot Island and James Island to the northeast.

The Calabar made for peaceful surroundings, with thick jungle right up to the riverbanks and balmy tropical temperatures. Roberts must have been confident in the strength of his flotilla and crew, because while the river entrance he was behind and the quiet anchorage he was now enjoying offered a degree of concealment and safety, they also made for a perfect trap.

Roberts's prolific raiding as he sailed south had left a trail of wreckage and witnesses that was being evaluated by Captain Chaloner Ogle of the HMS *Swallow*, who was now hunting Roberts and his pirate fleet.

The HMS *Swallow* was a fifty-gun fourth-rate ship of the line, which made it approximately equivalent to a frigate; it sported a line of guns between decks (the gun deck) and another on deck (the upper gun deck, quarterdeck and forecastle). It was built in 1703 but had been refitted to new specifications in 1719, just before departing on West Africa patrol. Notable among *Swallow*'s improvements were twenty-two massive "18-pounder" cannon—capable of firing large projectiles at long range—located on the gun deck. Between it gunnery, size and well-trained crew, the HMS *Swallow* was a dangerous adversary for Roberts' flotilla, even though it was outnumbered ship to ship.

However, for some military strategists, the term *outnumbered* defines a simple tactical situation easily remedied by appropriate countermeasures. Such countermeasures were about be engaged by the wily Captain Ogle, who arrived in the Calabar River area aboard the HMS *Sparrow* on February 5, 1722.

It is possible that Captain Ogle may have had some prior intelligence that there were three pirate ships in the river, with two of them being of considerable size and armament, because what happened next could have been a well-calculated move to divide Roberts's forces or simply a captain's quick response in avoiding a shoal.

With gun ports sealed shut and possibly flying a merchantman's ensign as a ruse, Captain Ogle sailed the HMS *Swallow* in full view of the river entrance but far enough away from Roberts's anchorage so that his ship couldn't be made out plainly. (Here is where some reports say Captain Ogle attempted to enter the river mouth but veered off to avoid a shoal. Arguably, it is hard to believe an experienced seaman like Captain Ogle would need to engage in this maneuver at a well-known port that he may have visited previously.)

Members of the Roberts's crew must have seen what appeared at a distance to be a large merchant ship under sail—likely lucrative prey. Roberts immediately mobilized the men of his consort ship, the *Ranger*, under the command of James Skyrme, and sent them to capture the prize.

The phrase low-speed pursuit would well define the sailing tactics of the time, when it often took days or weeks of expert maneuvering for one ship to overtake another, using the wind alone for propulsion and maneuverability. The wind could also be a weapon if one vessel deprived an opposing vessel of access.

So it was no surprise or concern to the pirates aboard *Ranger* that the vessel they considered to be a fat merchantman was leading them on a merry chase far out into the Gulf of Guinea.

On board the HMS *Swallow*, Captain Ogle must have let slip a sly smile as he lowered his spyglass while observing the ship pursuing him, all by itself, farther and farther away from the pirate flotilla's support.

According to several reports, at some point into the chase, far from shore, Captain Ogle took steps to slow his ship down without letting the pirates know his intentions. He may have ordered his helmsman to ease off the wind a bit or change course in a way his pursuers wouldn't consider suspicious, all the while quietly preparing his ship for battle. Most sources agree that the *Ranger* was able to close within cannon range and was just running up its black flag of piracy when the HMS *Swallow* ran up its English colors, opened its gun ports and ran out the guns. Captain Ogle would have likely turned his ship to face the *Ranger* broadside with a full complement of gunnery and "gaining the wind gauge" upwind of the *Ranger* to deny his opponent maneuverability. The pirates would have had only minutes to analyze and respond to their sudden change in fortune before the big guns of the HMS *Swallow* would have unleashed a fiery hell on them, sending hundreds of pounds of shot toward the *Ranger* and its now hapless crew.

Once the two ships engaged, the battle wouldn't have lasted long. Ten pirates were killed, and the *Ranger*'s captain, Skyrme, had his leg blown away by a cannonball, although he somehow remained on the deck and in command. His command was quickly terminated. The black flag was lowered and thrown overboard, while the *Ranger*'s crew prepared to submit to capture.

Having scored a victory over one pirate ship, Captain Ogle secured his vessel and his prisoners and prepared to return to the Calabar River and his primary target: Captain Bartholomew Roberts.

The morning of February 10, 1722, found Roberts's pirate crew celebrating the capture of a merchant vessel, the *Neptune*, that may have sailed right into their grasp at their cozy anchorage on the Calabar. Captain

Bartholomew Roberts's crew members were not allowed to drink onboard his ships. This illustration depicts crew members imbibing ashore near the Calabar River mouth prior to the engagement with HMS *Swallow*. *Public domain.*

Hill of the *Neptune* was apparently unconcerned over his circumstances, as he was joining Captain Roberts for breakfast on the *Royal Fortune*. The two captains were dining on salmagundi, the general description for a plate of pickled items often enhanced with whatever salted meat was aboard and/or fresh items from shore.

Many of Roberts's crew were still on shore celebrating their latest victory over the *Neptune* with their own favorite breakfast of intoxicating beverages, which, by order of Captain Roberts, were not allowed on board the *Royal Fortune*.

According to one report, there were storm clouds moving in under the balmy African skies.

Roberts must have been wondering about the *Ranger*, which had gone in pursuit of the apparent merchant ship some five days ago, so it was probably with pleasant surprise that Roberts received word from his lookouts that a ship was approaching the mouth of the Calabar River, the entrance to their anchorage. He must have assumed it was the *Ranger* returning victoriously. Then the lookouts noticed the vessel was flying French colors, so the pirates were perhaps looking forward to the possibility of yet more prey sailing into their midst.

One crewman, Robert Armstrong, a deserter from the HMS *Swallow* who had joined Roberts's crew, began to take special interest in the approaching ship. Its lines and configuration seemed familiar to him as the vessel came closer and more clearly in view.

The other pirates, many of whom were less than sober, paid little attention to the approaching vessel, and the atmosphere on the *Royal Fortune* and surrounding shoreline remained festive.

Once again, Captain Ogle and his capability for subterfuge were lulling his pirate prey into complacency. Even when Armstrong recognized his old ship and warned Roberts, he was still disregarded. The disguised Royal Navy vessel, flying its false colors, continued slowly sailing upriver, along the same channel described earlier, toward the anchored pirate flotilla, closing in on its prey. Meanwhile, the clouds overhead continued to darken.

While observations regarding the weather could be located in the historical record, as told in this account, there was no mention in these observations regarding the wind direction, which was all-important to sail-driven warships. We can only judge that Captain Ogle wouldn't have tried to make the Calabar River passage without a favorable breeze, which would have meant a prevailing southeasterly wind. This would have driven the HMS *Swallow* neatly through the river mouth and into the anchorage, probably close to Parrot Island, in an effort to block the pirate from making the outward channel. However, one report from *A General History of the Pyrates* described "the wind not favoring" the king's ship. Ogle may have decided that his best tactic was to drive the *Royal Fortune* into a battle that would have them both alongside and on the same heading, east by north, across the anchorage. This would allow him longer contact with Roberts, which was clearly at the pirate's disadvantage.

At about 10:30 a.m., in what was to become known as the Battle of Cape Lopez, Captain Ogle judged the trap was set and shed all essence of disguise, running out the HMS *Swallow*'s guns and hoisting the king's colors.

It became apparent to Roberts that Armstrong had been correct, and that battle with the well-armed HMS *Swallow* was now imminent. An alarm was sounded, and groggy pirates on shore took a last swig and headed back to their flagship. Roberts retired to his cabin and dressed in his stylish battle garb, including the gem-studded golden cross.

Upon returning to deck, resplendent in his red-hued finery and armed with his sword and four pistols, Captain Roberts evaluated his situation.

There would be little maneuverability in the small, shallow harbor, surrounded on all sides by shoals and terrain. He looked over his crew in disappointment as they drunkenly made their way back aboard, likely pitching, stumbling and cursing (although the cursing would have been under their breath, as Roberts didn't allow foul language on board).

He found Armstrong and inquired about the HMS *Swallow*'s capabilities in maneuvering and speed. He learned its large size would hamper both options. He already knew the HMS *Swallow*'s gunnery completely outclassed his own, and he knew the well-trained English tars manning those guns would be dead sober and deadly accurate—unlike his own crew.

Based on the engagement that followed, it appeared Roberts decided his best course of action would be to use his advantages in speed and maneuverability to minimize his battle time as much as possible. He would wait for the opposing ship to enter the small harbor and then sail his ship right by it, certainly suffering at least one broadside while delivering one of his own. With any luck, his vessel would survive the broadside in sailable condition, and he would ride the storm current down the channel and out to sea, leaving the larger, heavier English warship in his wake as it tried to come about and regain the wind to take up pursuit. With any luck, the HMS *Swallow* would go aground on one of the many shoals.

Roberts was likely sure that if he could make open water, he could make a run for safety and perhaps live to fight another day. He ordered his crew to lay on sail and cut the anchor cable to his ship. He left the crew of the *Little Ranger* to fare for themselves. He ran out the *Royal Fortune*'s guns and began closing distance on the Royal Navy ship.

By now, the surrounding clouds had grown dark and heavy with rain. Rumbles of thunder could be heard in the distance, and lightning flashes painted the dark clouds in violent flashes of electricity. The battle about to unfold would be fought in high winds and heavy rainfall, with bolts of weather-generated lightning streaking through the cloud-darkened sky, according to an observation at the time, which also described a "small tornado" blowing through the river valley.

Roberts must have considered his chances for survival when he turned to a nearby crew member, identified by one source as Richard Kennedy, and reminded Kennedy of Roberts's long-standing order that should he fall in battle—his body, weapons, jewelry and fine trappings—all be cast over the side of the vessel and lost to the sea.

According to the statement on record, made by the captain and crew of the HMS *Swallow*, at about 11:00 a.m., with the *Royal Fortune* "being within pistol shot abreast of us," the navy vessel fired a horrendous broadside that was immediately returned by the pirates, but "without equal damage."

The English narrative describes the *Royal Fortune*'s "mizzen [rear] topmast falling and some of their rigging being disabled" by this first volley of heavy lead cannonballs and flesh-piercing small rounds of grapeshot.

This damage would have hampered the pirates a bit but was far from disabling, which was confirmed by the English description of the action. "The pirate sailing better than us, shot ahead above half gun shot, while we continued firing, without intermission, such guns as we could bring to bear," the officers declared in their statement.

At this point in the battle, there are some descriptions that the helmsman on the *Royal Fortune* was having difficulty keeping on course, perhaps faltering in his progress to escape, or indicating damage to his maneuvering system. Mention should also be made that a favorable wind for Captain Ogle's entry at the Calabar River mouth would have meant that any vessels seeking to escape, such as the *Royal Fortune*, would be sailing upwind, at an extreme disadvantage, instead depending on the river current to gain the sea.

The English officers wrote: "By favour of the wind, we came alongside again, and exchanging a few more shot, about half past one [the time], his main [middle] mast came down, being shot away a little below the parrel." (A parrel is a loop of rope or steel fashioned to join a yard or gaff, which are used to hoist and control the sails.)

Pirates and Lost Treasure of Coastal Maine

To have the mast blown away at this low elevation would have taken out all of the sails for this mast, leaving the *Royal Fortune* with only the sails on its foremast to power the vessel. At this point, apparently still upriver from a strong current, the *Royal Fortune* would have been nearly "dead in the water" and the battle all but lost.

For Captain Bartholomew Roberts, the fight was already done, and his prophecy of "a short life but a merry one" was to end in fulfillment. As the acrid pall of weapon smoke wafted over the *Royal Fortune*, amid shattered rigging, the pitiful screams of the wounded and continuing gunfire, the well-dressed Captain Roberts lay dead. His neck was pierced by small lead balls called grapeshot or canister, which were fired in volume from a cannon, like a massive shotgun.

The weather continued to rage, and the hellish scene of smoke and blood was periodically accented by sheets of tropical rainfall—a final baptism for the pious pirate.

On the decks of *Royal Fortune*, the crew, with ears ringing from cannon fire, still uncomfortably drunk from their shore leave, were uncoordinated and ineffective in further defense. Their world began to collapse in the kind of slow-motion dream-like state that goes with disassociation from battle shock.

Following the captain's orders, Kennedy prepared to heave Roberts's body into the sea, until his attention focused on the golden cross, embedded with shining gemstones, still hanging from Roberts's neck. Presumably looking about furtively, Kennedy snatched the cross away, hiding it on his person until he could conceal it with his belongings. He then, with the help of other pirates, committed their captain's body into the water somewhere near the mouth of the Calabar River.

The slow outbound current, surging downriver from the rainfall runoff, must have gently carried the well-dressed remains of the pirate captain, cradled in the river depths, out into the Gulf of Guinea, the open ocean and finally the freedom Roberts was seeking in the final moments of his life.

The pirates struck their colors at 2:00 p.m., according to the English officers. The buccaneers on the *Royal Fortune* and the *Little Ranger*, over two hundred in all, surrendered. Upon his return to England, Captain Ogle was knighted for defeating Roberts.

However, the voyage of the jewel-studded golden cross, now in Kennedy's possession, was in just the very first stage of a journey that was destined for Maine.

According to W.C. Jameson in his book *Buried Treasures of New England*, Richard Kennedy, now a prisoner, requested an audience with Captain

Ogle. When the two met, Kennedy offered to lead the captain or his agents to a number of locations where Roberts buried treasure—if appropriate arrangements could be made.

It may be of interest to the reader that very few pirates were known to have buried treasure, in spite of popular belief. Most pirates would share out their hoard with the crew at the end of a voyage, and then it was every man for himself. However, in Roberts's case, in possession of valuables from four hundred ships taken during his career, and no end in sight to his voyage, it would have made sense to lighten his load on occasion and leave some hidden stashes to revisit later. Removing treasure from the ship would also reduce temptation on the part of individual crew members to steal some of the goods or, worse yet, for the crew to mutiny and make off with the entire haul.

In any case, Jameson wrote that a deal was struck, and a treasure recovery expedition was launched with Kennedy as the guide. Somehow, Kennedy was able to keep the gem-studded golden cross in his possession and to profit from some of the recovered valuables, ending the voyage with four small chests in his possession. Reaching the American Atlantic Seaboard at an undocumented date, he purchased a sloop and sailed, single-handedly, north to find a quiet place to settle down, which he did in the area of modern-day Boothbay, Maine. He found an abandoned homestead located on a lonely peninsula and moved into a rock-built structure there.

At this point, his four boxes of treasure would have become quite a burden to him. There was no such thing as a bank in early Boothbay. In order to keep them safe, he would have had to keep them in his sight at all times. There was only one option: he would have to find a place to hide them.

According to Jameson, Kennedy loaded the chests into his sloop and took a number of days to explore the area, seeking a good spot to stash them. Finally, he found a place he described as a "bay" on the nearby lower Kennebec River, where he withdrew enough coins to live on, quite comfortably by his current standards, for several years. He then dug a hole about four feet deep, placed the chests in it, and laid a flat stone over them, before filling the hole in. He stripped some bark off a nearby tree and used his knife to carve a simple map into it.

Upon returning to Boothbay, he purchased a sheet of vellum, which in those times was made with processed calfskin, unlike modern imitation vellum, which is made from rag cotton or interior tree bark fibers. Most important documents of the day were created on vellum, which had archival quality. Using the notes on his bark carving and a recollection of the area, he drew a detailed map of the treasure site, as told by Jameson.

Pirates and Lost Treasure of Coastal Maine

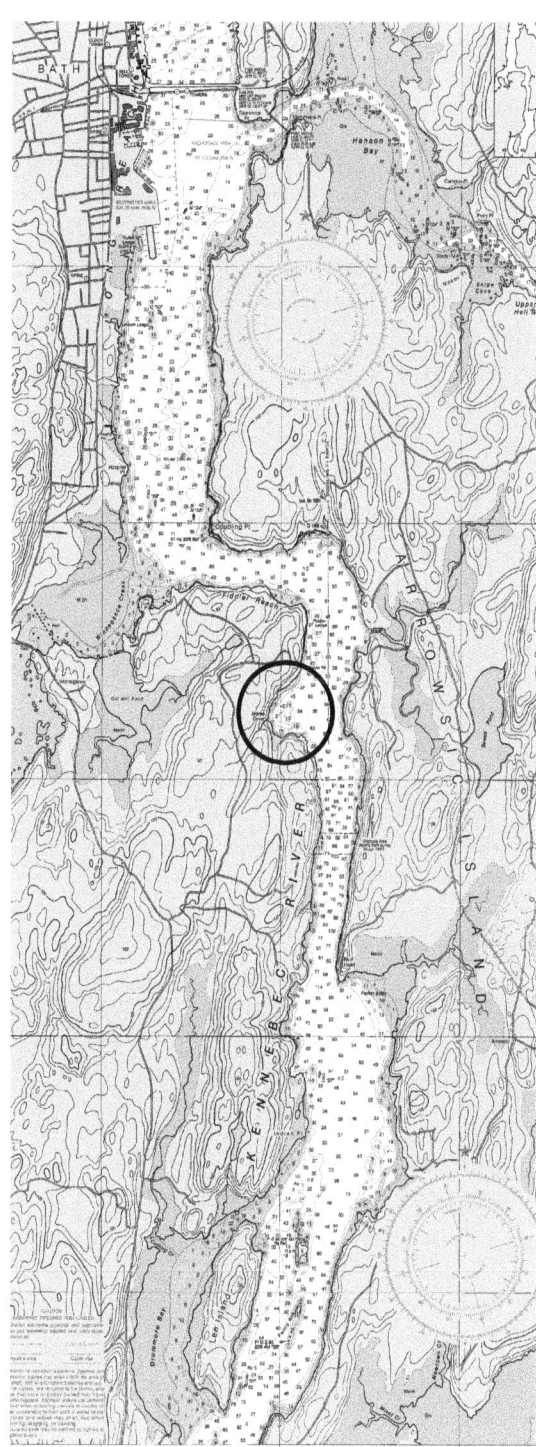

The Kennebec River in Midcoast Maine, with Morse Cove in the circled area. Morse Cove best matches the description of a "bay" described in a treasure map leading to hidden treasure. *United States Geological Survey.*

Soon bored with life in Maine, Richard Kennedy returned to England, according to Jameson, where he was executed by authorities who learned of his pirate past. He left a small sea chest with a pirate friend known only as "Booth." In that chest was, among other pirate curiosities, Kennedy's vellum treasure map. After examining the contents of the chest and finding the map nothing but confusing gibberish, Booth turned the box and its contents over to a relative, as told by Jameson. The chest was handed down for generations and finally fell into the possession of one Terrence Booth, who recognized the map for the path to treasure it was intended to be and determined to find, for himself, the pirate hoard. In 1879, Booth took his savings, packed some belongings, including the small chest, and set sail for America.

Upon his arrival on the American coast, he quickly went through his savings and subsisted on menial jobs, all the while trying to figure out what river was depicted on the map. By 1882, he had become weary of lugging the chest around and paid a small sum to a woman, Emeline Benner Lewis, to store the chest in her attic until he could return for it, Jameson wrote.

Here is where Jameson's 1998 narrative begins to match a much earlier narrative—that of prolific author Edward Rowe Snow in his 1944 book *Pirates and Buccaneers of the Atlantic Coast*, later republished with updates by Jeremy D'Entremont in 2004.

Emeline Benner Lewis stayed true to her promise, keeping Booth's chest safely in her attic and never allowing anyone to inspect it, especially her nephew George Frederick Benner, who was full of youthful curiosity about the mysterious container. As time went by, Terrence Booth never returned, and while young George Benner reached adulthood, he never lost his childish curiosity about the chest, inquiring about it every time he visited his aunt. Finally, Emeline concluded that after eighteen years of absence, Booth must have perished somewhere. When George visited again, circa 1900, he at last got his wish—he could have the chest and whatever contents were within.

Likely finding a spot at his aunt's table, he carefully raised the lid and looked over his find. The contents, according to the combined reports of Jameson and Snow, included an old quadrant, a whale's tooth, a copy of *The Pirate* by Walter Scott and several letters, one dated 1830 from Bristol, England. (One must wonder, at this juncture of the story, if the quadrant, a navigational device, may have been originally owned by Bartholomew Roberts, a trained navigator.)

However, it was a piece of folded vellum that drew George's ever-present curiosity. As the young man unfolded the parchment, his eyes must have

The northern section of Morse Cove in Phippsburg, where some of Bartholomew Roberts's lost treasure may still remain hidden. *Author photo.*

widened at the hand-drawn map. Boston-raised, George was already familiar with the New England coastline and was able to recognize on the map Casco Bay in southern Maine. Following the coastal lines farther north, he recognized the river mouths of the mid coast, and especially the larger Kennebec River. He noted with interest a small bay in the lower Kennebec marked with a star. Under the star were these directions: "Stand abrest quartsbolder bring top in line with hill N 1/2 m it lise 12 fathom N E near big trees under stone."

Roughly translated, the phrase would most likely read: "Stand abreast quartz boulder, bring top in line with hill North ½ mile, it lies 12 fathoms [72 feet] northeast near big trees under stone."

George had caught the treasure bug. He found a friend with similar drive, and they began saving money for an expedition to Maine, most likely leaving in the fall of 1901, hoping to find the treasure before winter snow began to fly.

They rented a sloop and sailed to Boothbay, finding a place to tie up for the night. The following morning, they sailed out of Boothbay, most likely around the Southport peninsula and Georgetown Island before sailing north up the Kennebec River.

Their eyes searching the shoreline, they found a bay, and in that bay, they were able to make out a large boulder encrusted with sparkling quartz, perhaps the "quartz boulder" mentioned in the treasure map, and they excitedly put to shore. They searched for the "big trees" as described on the map but were only able to find a single tree. The afternoon was settling into evening, and it was a fair distance back to their safe mooring, so they ended their efforts for the day and returned to Boothbay.

The next morning, full of fresh energy, they returned to the quartz boulder and redoubled their efforts. This time, they examined the area around the lone tree and found the remaining stump of another large tree near the one still standing. Suspecting these might be the trees described in the map, they began using a crowbar they had brought along to systematically thrust into the earth, in hopes of striking something solid underground.

After some effort, they could feel the steel tip on the crowbar scrape against stone. Their excitement must have been palpable. They dug into the soil and found several flat rocks. Heaving them up out of the ground, they revealed the damaged lid of a wooden chest. With some more exploration, they found another damaged wooden chest. Peering through the damage of both chests, they saw a large cache of coins. Reaching in with their hands,

Small boulders at Morse Cove in Phippsburg, many of them with quartz or quartz-like deposits as described on the boulder in the treasure map. *Author photo.*

they scooped handfuls of the coins, discolored by age. By the coins' color and weight, it was obvious that they were gold. The treasure hunters also noticed a roll of canvas wrapped around some objects, and when they unrolled the bundle, they discovered a pearl necklace and a gem-studded gold cross nine inches in length. Could it have been the gold cross so revered by pirate Captain Bartholomew Roberts, carried from the battle at Calabar all the way to Maine by the opportunistic Richard Kennedy? There will never be any way to prove it, but given the narrative laid down on these pages, with the point-to-point description of its potential journey, the possibility that perhaps it was cannot be entirely ruled out. And there is a modern revelation yet to come in a story that is not quite finished.

Benner and his friend, worried about the security of their newfound riches, sailed the shortest route to Boston, arriving at the Northern Avenue Public Landing two days later. They immediately made arrangements with a bank and delivered their hoard, which returned the sum of $20,000, a sizable amount during that era. At this point, the cross was lost to time, and while it may still exist somewhere, there is no official record of it.

Unfortunately for the two treasure seekers, there was no reference in the map that four chests were buried along the Kennebec, not just the two they were able to recover. Does that mean there may be two chests still concealed underground at the location? Once again, a mystery that may never be resolved.

When one examines a modern-day chart of the Kennebec River, there is only one location on the lower river that matches the description of "a small bay": Morse Cove on the west bank of the river just south of a section known as Fiddler's Reach. A portion of the northern part of the cove is open to the public as a boat landing, which makes it easy to access. The southern part of the cove is private property and not accessible to the public.

Most certainly, all of the landmarks described in the original treasure map are either altered or gone. However, once the visitor begins to explore the shoreline at the town landing, the number of rocks encrusted with quartz or quartz-like deposits becomes apparent. Could these be evidence of the possibility that a large quartz rock like the one described in the map could have once existed here?

For whatever answers may be extrapolated about the journey of the bejeweled golden cross, based on historical notations, from the Caribbean to Nova Scotia and then on to West Africa before Richard Kennedy was apparently able to spirit it away to Maine, there are also many unanswered questions.

This close-up of a rock from Morse Cove in Phippsburg shows the quartz or quartz-like deposits found on many of the rocks in the area. *Author photo.*

Perhaps the cross will surface somewhere, someday, as proof of its existence and history. Or perhaps an excavation crew in the vicinity of Morse Cove will accidentally unearth the remains of two wooden chests, spilling out their priceless treasure. Certainly the most likely scenario is that, like the pirate captain whose body was committed to the dark, deep currents of the sea and never recovered, both the cross and the treasure will remain forever lost, but never forgotten.

7

DISASTER AND DISAPPOINTMENT FOR BLACK SAM BELLAMY'S CREW

The idea of Caribbean swashbucklers in a pirate flotilla carrying a vast treasure is not an image one usually associates with Midcoast Maine. History tells us differently with the story of Black Sam Bellamy and his band of sea robbers destined for Damariscove Island offshore of Midcoast Maine in April 1717.

Bellamy was northbound after a year spent on pirate raids throughout the Caribbean. He was sailing with his captains Paulsgrave Williams, commanding the *Marianne*, a mid-sized sloop that had been part of the pirate fleet, and Richard Noland, commanding the recently captured *Ann Galley*, a type of small merchant vessel called a snow with a displacement of ten tons.

Bellamy's flagship was the three-hundred-ton galley *Whydah*. He had taken the *Whydah* by force after a long chase and turned the former slave runner into one of the most formidable fighting ships from the western Caribbean to the Gulf of Maine.

It was also carrying more treasure than many a pirate had ever seen. Bellamy had captured in excess of fifty prizes, and all of that loot—an estimated four and a half tons of coins, jewels and more—was stowed away safely in the *Whydah*'s hold, under Black Sam's watchful eye.

Some of the treasure was secured in an innovative way. The *Whydah*'s hold included a number of cannon barrels that, while not presently in use, were removed from their carriages and stowed below decks, making for an effective ballast to keep the ship upright. Some of these cannon barrels also made very secure plunder lockers. Valuables were placed in the empty barrel, and then the gun muzzle was sealed shut with molten lead, which made pilfering an impossibility. Cannon barrels used this way have been on display at the Whydah Pirate Museum in Massachusetts.

As the hot summer and the hurricane season began to loom, Black Sam ordered his flotilla north. Both the *Whydah* and the *Marianne* were in need of repairs that Bellamy planned on making somewhere in Midcoast Maine. Along the way, Bellamy was said to have plans to meet with a certain girl he left behind in Cape Cod named Maria Hallett. Before gaining the American East Coast, he conferred with his captains, and the decision was made that should their ships be separated (a very good possibility), they would meet at Damaries Cove Island off the coast of Maine (now known as Damariscove.)

No one knows for sure why Bellamy picked the tiny island off Maine's shore. The Maine coast was still wild, and Damaries Cove would have been known to seafarers as a longtime seasonal fishing station. There has also been speculation about a pirate settlement near the Machias River that Bellamy may have been headed for. (See chapter 5, "Pirate Treasure in Machias.")

What is known from depositions, court testimony and various reports is that Bellamy's flotilla sailed coastwise on a northerly course up the Atlantic Seaboard. At some point, Paulsgrave Williams, aboard the *Marianne*, took leave of the flotilla to visit his family at Block Island offshore of Rhode Island—then considered a pirate haven where ill-gotten gains were often sold off at auction in the port.

Bellamy continued north–northeast aboard the *Whydah*, with Noland and the *Ann Galley*, taking prey as opportunity allowed. On April 26, 1717, off the coast of Massachusetts, Bellamy's crew took the *Mary Anne* (all of these similar names are coincidental), a two-masted merchant vessel known as a pink, with holds full of wine. Later that day, a small coasting sloop, the *Fisher*, was taken after it sailed right into the midst of the pirate fleet. Prize crews were promptly put aboard each vessel, and the flotilla continued well offshore—until Bellamy ordered a course change toward shore just before nightfall.

As darkness enveloped the northbound group of vessels, a freshening breeze rose from due east. Raging winds of a storm gathered, and as midnight approached, the four vessels now associated with Bellamy's flotilla were all in dire straits. Square-rigged ships are not made for traveling upwind, and so the easterly gale drove the *Whydah*, the *Ann Galley* and the *Mary Anne* toward the lee shore of Cape Cod. The *Fisher*'s sloop rigging allowed it more options for beating to windward, so it must have fared just a bit better than the larger ships.

A depiction of the *Anne* under the command of Richard Nolan and a prize ship, the *Fisher*. The *Anne* survived the storm that sank the *Whydah*, while the *Fisher* was badly damaged and had to be scuttled. *Whydah Pirate Museum.*

At some point, the three larger ships became separated, and the *Fisher* fell in with the *Ann Galley* in the hope of weathering the coming storm with the safety of the sturdier vessel nearby. The *Ann Galley* and the *Fisher* were both still some distance out from the savage breakers and deadly shoreline. Both set anchors in hopes that they could ride out the storm "on the hook."

However, the *Whydah* and the *Mary Anne* were caught too far inshore when the storm hit.

The sailors and pirates on the wine-laden *Mary Anne* had already consumed a fair share of its cargo, which may have imparted some liquid courage, as they decided that instead of weathering the storm afloat they would run their ship up on the sandy beach and hope for the best. Bringing the vessel about as the storm raged around them, they pointed it toward shore and held on as the gale force winds filled the ship's remaining sails, driving it to surf through the enormous waves and run its bow up on the sandy beach of Pochet Island, near the Wellfleet area of Cape Cod. The crew scrambled to the decks and used hatchets and cutlasses to hack away the *Mary Anne*'s masts and rigging, leaving the sea to pound over the hull. They returned to the cabin of the beached vessel, where they secured the hatches against the relentless, storm-driven surf, and became suddenly religious under the guidance of a literate sailor who read hymns from the Bible. Sailors and pirates alike eagerly finished off more of the alcoholic cargo as massive waves pounded the ship's timbers over their heads through the night.

Farther north, the crew of the *Whydah* had no opportunity to beach their vessel and sing a few hymns over wine. The ship's load of cannon and treasure gave it greater weight and deeper draft. The crew may have tried to drop anchors and hold fast, and with this failing, they may have made a desperate attempt to turn the ship bow first into the approaching beach—a much safer approach than crashing stern first.

The now terrified crew of the *Whydah* found that their best efforts were to end in vain. At around midnight, the elegantly outfitted warship, along with some 160 men and the riches aboard, hit the sand bars stern-first off modern-day Wellfleet, Massachusetts. *Whydah* lost its main mast and began to break up immediately in the raging surf and pitch-black darkness. The force of the storm against the grounded ship was remarkable, as evidenced by the remains found of one pirate who had a pewter plate embedded in his shoulder blade. The once proud galley was pounded to splinters in the surf, the crew thrown into the sea and vast treasure scattered to the sandy depths.

Sheets of rain continued to fall until the weather slowly yielded to scant beams of sunshine filtered by the remaining storm clouds, eerily lighting the gruesome scene on the morning of April 27. The crew aboard the beached *Mary Anne* found that they were badly hungover but alive. They stumbled from the battered hulk and found a nearby tavern; there they celebrated their deliverance and were arrested a short time later.

Several miles north, only two ragged survivors of the *Whydah*'s destruction pulled themselves to shore. The surf and the beach around them were littered with pieces of the proud ship and the bodies of drowned pirates. Both of these survivors were later arrested.

Offshore, the crews of the ships under Captain Noland's command emerged from below decks to find that their anchors had held and their lives had been spared. The *Ann Galley* had weathered the storm well, but the smaller *Fisher* was badly damaged. Its prize, crew and prisoners were transferred to the *Ann Galley*, according to a deposition later given by captured *Fisher* crew members Ralph Merry and Samuel Roberts. *Fisher*'s hatches were opened to the weather and sea in hopes that it would soon sink, and the little sloop was set adrift.

With the *Ann Galley* ready to make sail, Noland likely scanned the horizon and the visible coastline but could find no sign of the *Whydah*. By midmorning,

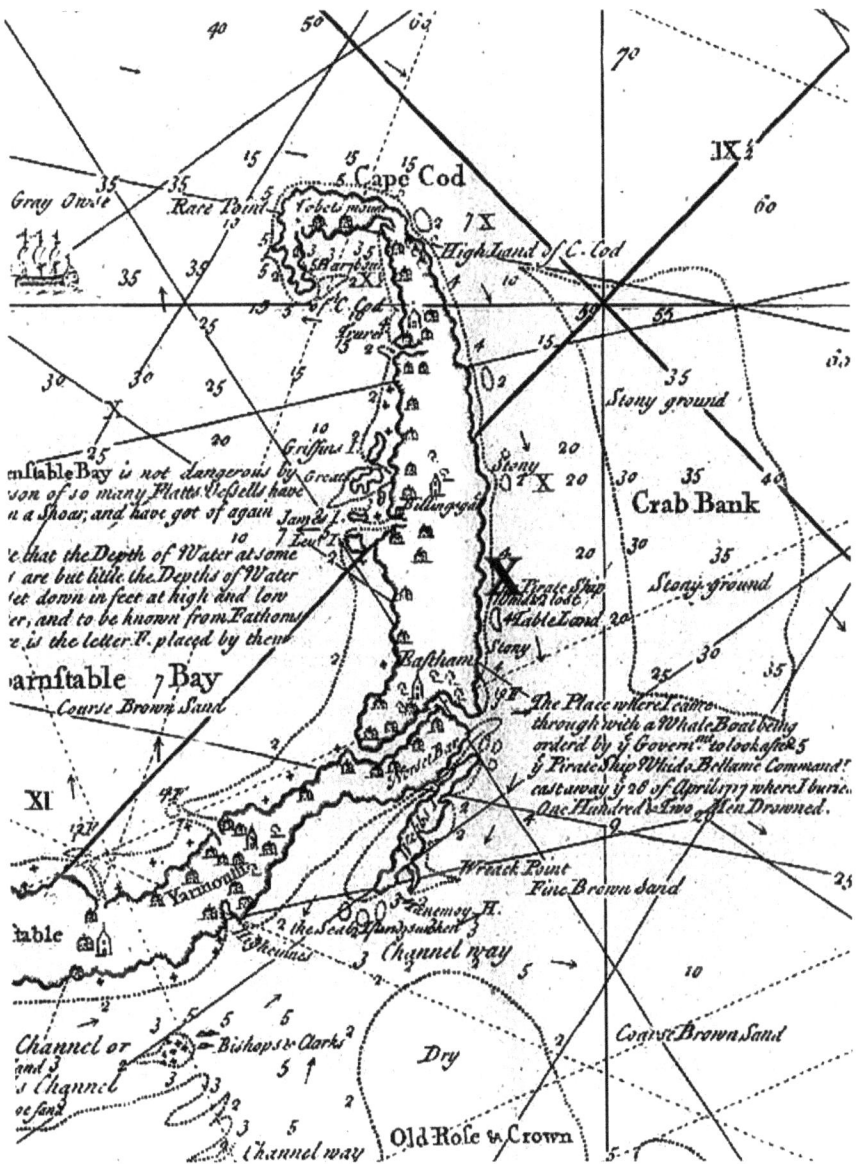

The location of the *Whydah*, marked with an X, as shown in a 1734 map documenting salvage and victim burial efforts at the time. *Cyprian Southack, Library of Congress.*

Left: The ship's bell that confirmed the wreckage being explored by Barry Clifford and Expedition *Whydah* off Wellfleet, Massachusetts, was indeed that of the treasure ship *Whydah*. *Author photo, bell courtesy of the Whydah Pirate Museum.*

Below: A detail of the ship's bell recovered from wreckage offshore of Wellfleet, Massachusetts, clearly identifies the vessel as "Whydah Galley." *Photo by the author, bell courtesy of the Whydah Pirate Museum.*

the wind had shifted to westerly, which would allow the *Ann Galley* to safely navigate. Assuming that the larger *Whydah* had survived, Noland weighed anchor, ordered his crew aloft to set sails and turned his bow northward toward the meeting place at Damaries Cove and Maine. Noland and his entire crew hoped for the best—all of their plunder from a year's worth of raiding was aboard the *Whydah*.

To the south, Paulsgrave Williams aboard the *Marianne* had earlier departed Block Island and found a cozy bay at Gardiner Island near New York to weather out the storm that took the *Whydah*. With the weather clearing, he raised sail and set his course for the pirate rendezvous at Damaries Cove and the big payday when he was sure the treasure aboard the *Whydah* was to be divided among the crews.

Noland's ship made good time, and only two days later, on April 29, he dropped anchor at Monhegan Island. It is unknown why Noland decided to bypass Damaries Cove. Perhaps being the first to arrive sent a suspicious chill through the veteran pirate's bones. Logically, the *Whydah* should have already been there. Moreover, as a cautious buccaneer, Noland may have shied away from the shallow harbor at Damaries Cove, as it had only one point of entry and exit. While the harbor at Monhegan was a bit rougher, and the rocky bottom made it hard to anchor, the hideaway had two points of ingress and egress. The island also had a freshwater pond and two high points for a lookout: one on Monhegan and the other at nearby Manana Island, located just yards away on the west side of the harbor.

The same day Noland anchored at Monhegan, Williams was taking his time to the rendezvous, lingering about Long Island Sound and taking targets of opportunity. It wasn't until daybreak on May 17 that Williams's lookouts spotted the headland of Cape Elizabeth and the *Marianne* was finally in Maine waters.

A report at the time from Captain John Lane to Governor Samuel Shute of Massachusetts and New Hampshire (a territory that then included Maine) described how the sloop *Elizabeth* was taken near the Spurwink area of Maine by Williams as he headed north in the *Marianne*.

Several days later, pirates aboard the *Marianne* captured a small fishing vessel and found that one of its crew members could guide them to Damaries Cove. The course was set, and Williams was soon dropping anchor at Damaries Cove.

The *Piscataqua (NH) Dispatch* reported, "Fishermen tell us that the Pirate Sloop *Marianne* of 8 guns left Richmond's Island last Lord's Day [May 19, 1717] and others tell us that both the Pirate Sloops *Marianne* and *Elizabeth* are together at Damerill's Cove [*sic*] careening and that one of them has about 90 men on board her."

Richmond's Island (now known as Richmond Island) is located about one mile south of Cape Elizabeth in Maine and was a known stopover for sea rovers, most likely because of a freshwater pond located there. In the late 1600s, the pirate Dixie Bull was thought to have stopped over at this semiforested offshore isle, so it is no surprise that Williams, and likely other

PIRATES AND LOST TREASURE OF COASTAL MAINE

The sunken remains shown here in York, Maine, are those of a two-masted vessel called a pink or pinque. These were standard cargo ships that could compare in size to the "snow" under the command of Richard Noland. These surprisingly tough little vessels were favorites of pirates and were common along the Eastern Seaboard of America and into the Caribbean. *Photograph courtesy of Detective M. Kalcina, York Police Department.*

pirate captains, knew of the place. In 1855, a farmer reportedly plowed up twenty-one pieces of gold and thirty-one pieces of silver on the island, which many people attribute to Dixie Bull. Of course, such a stash could have been left by any seafarer over the years. (For the complete story on Dixie Bull, including a description of how the public can visit Richmond Island, see chapter 3, "Dixie Bull, Maine's First Pirate.")

Unknown to the pirates, they were being stalked by a pirate hunter—according to a report in the *Piscataqua Dispatch*. Colonel Shadrach Walton had been previously "sent out from hence in quest of the Pirates"; however, "we have heard nothing as yet" in regard to his progress. Perhaps fortunately for Colonel Walton, given the number and considerable armament of the pirates, there are no reports he ever engaged Williams or Noland and their cohorts.

The *Marblehead (MA) Dispatch* mentioned the *Ann Galley* (in the article written as the *Anne*) operating in the area of Monhegan Island (located about fifteen miles due east of Damaries Cove), as described by the crew of a small fishing boat having returned to port. The fishermen described the *Ann Galley* accurately, as a snow (a ship-rigged, two-masted vessel) with a crew of eighteen. They were detained by the pirates for "some time" and then released.

The article mentions the pirates taking a sloop out of Boston but offers no details. Also according to the article, Ralph Merry, a prisoner from the

Fisher, who was party to a deposition mentioned earlier in this chapter, was transferred to the fishing boat and sent ashore by the pirates at Monhegan.

Along with another witness in the deposition, Samuel Roberts, Merry later described Noland's crew aboard the *Ann Galley* as doing what pirates would do while waiting for the *Whydah*—plundering any vessels they encountered.

They describe Noland's crew as fitting out a long boat, manning it with a small crew of heavily armed pirates and dispatching it to Matinicus Island, about twenty-five miles east by north from Monhegan, in search of prey. Such a move speaks volumes about the confidence of these veteran seafarers, as the crossing from Monhegan to Matinicus is fraught with unpredictable weather and frequently high seas. Many a modern-day sailor would be wary of this journey in a small boat, complete with navigational and safety aids. The pirates made this run in an open rowboat, perhaps with the assistance of a sail.

Upon arriving at Matinicus, the detachment of buccaneers found targets aplenty, taking a shallop (small merchant vessel), a sloop and three schooners. They pilfered the schooners for compasses and sails and returned to Monhegan with the sloop and shallop. There, they fitted the sloop out as a new addition to their pirate fleet, staffing it with a crew of ten sea rovers.

The pirates pointed their sloop west by north and made sail to Pemaquid Harbor, about thirteen miles distant. There they found a sloop under Captain Carr and boarded it by force. The sloop was in poor condition, but the captain had knowledge of local navigation, so he was taken prisoner to be used as pilot and the crew returned to Monhegan, leaving the damaged sloop behind.

The pirates who stayed in Monhegan aboard the *Ann Galley* had also stayed busy, taking two shallops that wandered into the harbor.

There doesn't appear to be any specific documentation putting Williams's and Noland's crews together at the same place. However, according to Ken Kinkor of the Whydah Pirate Museum, the two crews apparently did meet in waters offshore of Midcoast Maine, which is certainly plausible given that both crews were operating only about fifteen miles apart. An exhibit at the museum describes some of the pirates "dispersing in Maine," and Kinkor believes that it's likely the two vessels crossed paths at some point, with the *Ann Galley* being abandoned, possibly near present-day Boothbay Harbor, and its crew joining the *Marianne*. Kinkor supports this theory with a report that in late spring of 1717, Williams and the *Marianne* visited New York City with more crew on board the ship than before he had visited Maine.

The coastline at Wellfleet, Massachusetts, near where the *Whydah* sank. *Author photo.*

What is known beyond any doubt is that at some point, the crews of both vessels decided there was no longer any use in waiting for the *Whydah* and realized that their big payday would never come to fruition.

As days became weeks and their combined journeys gravitated back to the buccaneer haunts of the Atlantic Seaboard, each of them would have learned of *Whydah*'s demise and the loss of some 160 of their crewmates. Many of them must have wondered about the fate of their riches, a treasure that is estimated to be worth $6 to $8 million in today's currency. While some of that treasure has been recovered and is now on public display at the Whydah Pirate Museum, most of it still lies under the ever-shifting sands offshore of Cape Cod, somewhat like the pirates lost in that horrific storm—vanished but not forgotten.

8

PIRATE DECEIT AND A MASSACRE AT FORT LOYALL

On any given day in the city of Portland, Maine, thousands of people will either walk or drive by the busy intersection of Fore and India Streets. Located near the waterfront, the area is home to unique restaurants, trendy shops and a new boutique hotel. During the summer and fall months, elegant ships are docked only several hundred yards away at the Ocean Gateway cruise terminal, with their many passengers rambling by the area as they make their way to the popular Old Port.

Unless these residents and visitors take the time to read a weathered brass plaque located on the corner of a nondescript brick building nearby, it is likely that none of them know they are strolling through the scene of a historic massacre in which over two hundred men, women and children were slaughtered at Fort Loyall and left in a gory heap. Even for those familiar with this history, the fact that pirates may have unwittingly contributed to this bloody defeat is a rarely reported fact.

The story began in 1689, when a group of Bostonians hatched a convoluted plot to entice the British warship HMS *Rose* out of the harbor by having a vessel masquerade as a pirate outside of the entrance channel. A local captain named Thomas Pound was appointed by the good citizens to rendezvous just outside the anchorage with a sloop under the command of Thomas Hawkins. They would create enough small incidents that the officers aboard the HMS *Rose* would feel compelled to make sail and leave Boston to pursue them. The scheme was part of a larger plan that involved a controversial change of power in England, allowing William and Mary

Visitors and residents stroll down a scenic walkway on Commercial Street and India Street in Portland, Maine, near the area once occupied by Fort Loyall. *Photo by Dominik Lobkowicz.*

to ascend to the throne, but none of that would matter in the end. Almost immediately upon boarding the sloop, followed by a group of heavily armed men, Pound became a real pirate, forcibly commandeering the ship and setting a northerly course toward Maine, in complete violation of his original mandate.

Just up the coast, Captain Pound came upon a ketch, the *Mary*, captured it and transferred his crew to the larger vessel, continuing on a northerly course.

Several days later, posing as a merchant vessel, they anchored the *Mary* near present-day Portland, within view of Fort Loyall. Continuing their ruse, three men from the *Mary*, led by John Darby, went ashore to fill water casks. While two men busied themselves with the task, Darby falsely told the fort commander that there was a wounded man aboard the *Mary* and inquired if there was a surgeon available. Surgeons were highly valued aboard pirate ships, and Darby had a plan to acquire one.

Indeed, there was a surgeon stationed at the fort. The doctor, accompanied the three men and their water casks, was rowed back to the *Mary*. Upon boarding, he was approached by Captain Pound, who invited him to join the crew and share in the spoils of the sweet trade. According to accounts, the good doctor was initially attracted to the offer but lost his nerve and declined in the end. Somewhat surprisingly, he wasn't forced into service by the pirates but allowed to return to the fort. He relayed his story to the officers, who formed a detail of seven men to provide an extra watch during the overnight hours, in case the pirates decided to come ashore. Unfortunately, the men selected to protect the garrison decided instead to join the rovers aboard the *Mary*.

Once the fort's company was fast asleep, the turncoats stealthily took as many of the soldiers' possessions as they could, as well as making off with much of the garrison's ammunition supply and a brass cannon barrel. Quietly, they loaded their goods onto a rowboat and made it aboard the *Mary* before the remaining loyal soldiers awoke and sounded the alarm. Once clear of the harbor, the sea robbers set a new southerly course, where they were next reported taking a Nantucket-bound sloop near Cape Cod.

Back at Fort Loyall, the garrison was now undermanned and understaffed, not to mention constantly under the threat of attack from Native Americans and the French. With the fall season approaching, a time when Native Americans often went on the offensive after their crops were harvested and before the first winter snowfall, desperate word was sent to Boston for reinforcements and supplies. A group of 250 men under the command of Benjamin Church arrived just in time, while a large group of Native Americans was forming up on a nearby island.

On September 21, 1689, the Native Americans paddled their canoes to the Back Cove area north of Fort Loyall and disembarked, moving along en masse toward the ridgeline where present-day Congress Street now runs. Somewhere in this vicinity, Church's men formed a line and opened fire on the approaching Native Americans. The fight was sharp and deadly, with twenty-one of the English militia killed. The casualty figures for Native Americans were not recorded. The English soldiers prevailed, and the Native Americans were driven from the area and back to their villages for the coming cold season.

However, the approaching winter also meant the departure of Church's company, as there were not enough provisions at the fort to support so large a group. As the chill of a Maine winter began to settle in, with gray

This building, presently housing the Gorham Savings Bank on India Street and Commercial Street, in Portland, Maine, has a plaque on the front left corner commemorating the fall of Fort Loyall. The fort was actually located about one block farther up India Street, near Fore Street, which was the waterfront in the 1600s. The Commercial Street area was created with landfill at a later date. *Photo by Dominik Lobkowicz.*

snow clouds drifting in over the forest, Fort Loyall remained dangerously unprepared, still short on the ammunition, artillery, and personnel that had sailed south with the pirates.

The winter was long for the small detachment of soldiers and an estimated two hundred civilians within the garrison's protection. Supplies were likely running short at Fort Loyall when the first signs of spring arrived in May 1690. A group of colonists were sent out to forage in the area of present-day Munjoy Hill and encountered elements from a large contingent of French and Native Americans. The colonists quickly retreated back to the safety of the fort, but their comfort was short-lived.

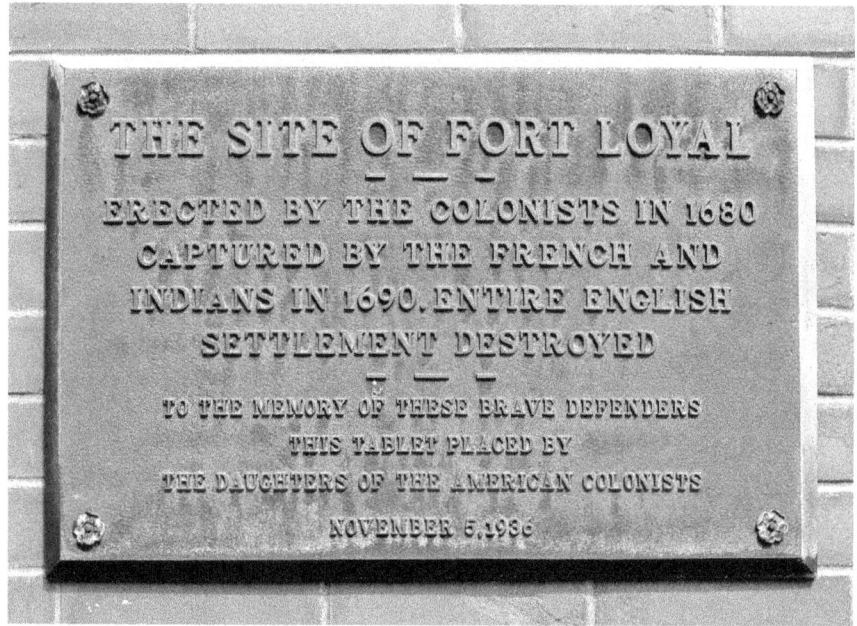

This plaque memorializes "these brave defenders" of Fort Loyall (referred to as Fort Loyal in modern times). It is located on a corner of the Gorham Savings Bank on India Street and Commercial Street in Portland, Maine. *Photograph by Dominik Lobkowicz.*

Some four to five hundred Native Americans and French, under the command of Joseph-François Hertel de la Fresnière and Baron St. Castin, soon surrounded the beleaguered outpost. The settlers held their garrison four days before accepting terms of surrender from the French that allowed them to walk back to Boston. However, the Native Americans didn't feel they were party to any such agreement, claiming they had legitimate grudges against the colonists. When the gate to Fort Loyall swung open, the Native Americans rushed in and massacred some two hundred civilians, including women and children. Some officers and soldiers were spared, to be held by the French as captives for purposes of trading or ransom. The fort and outbuildings were burned to the ground.

With no chance for the settlers to send word for help, it wasn't until summer had settled in that reinforcements arrived, only to find decomposing bodies and charred palisades. It is unknown how much difference the seven deserters to the pirate ship might have made in the defense of Fort Loyall, but the brass cannon also lost to the pirates could have certainly been a deciding factor. There are no reports that the attackers had any artillery, as transporting heavy guns through the muddy conditions of a Maine spring would have been an onerous task. Artillery fire, if it had been more available for defensive purposes, may well have had a devastating effect on the French and Native American attackers, not only through casualties but also in the sheer terror that falling shells can inspire.

Far from the nightmare at Fort Loyall, the pirates under Captain Pound may have never known about the two hundred horrible deaths their deceit may have caused.

9

RACHEL WALL, FEMALE TERROR OF THE STORMY SEAS

Rachel Wall, who reportedly terrorized the Isles of Shoals from 1781 to 1782, is the best-known female pirate associated with Maine. Rachel, along with her husband, George, and a small crew of soulless scoundrels, operated as wreckers, using a ruse to lure their victims to disaster, then killing them to the last sailor, leaving no witnesses.

Isles of Shoals, a group of small islands and tidal ledges located about six miles southeast of the Maine coast, is naturally treacherous. On blustery nights, when sea storms roil the water and wind-driven wave crests are taller that a sloop's main mast, these low-lying landfalls are nearly invisible until the moment a ship runs hard aground, sending a horrible shudder from the keel through the decks and up the rigging, dooming the vessel and its crew to the relentless waves on a frigid, rocky, storm-washed coastline.

Adding a group of predatory pirates to this mix is the stuff that mariners' nightmares are made of. Rachel and her gang had a favorite method to entice their victims, using the allure of a damsel in distress.

Aboard their stolen ship the *Essex*, they would take steps to give the vessel the appearance that it had been damaged in a storm. Then they would find a suitable spot to lie in wait until the weather took a turn for the worse. Upon spying likely prey passing by, they would make enough sail to close some distance while Rachel wailed and pleaded for help and the crew of brigands went into hiding.

When the target ship changed course and came alongside the *Essex*, eager to assist the stricken woman, heavily armed pirates would jump from

Pirates and Lost Treasure of Coastal Maine

Somewhat like the tactics used by Rachel Wall and her crew of wreckers, this illustration depicts pirates using men dressed as women and an ongoing party, complete with music, to lure a target ship within their grasp while the crew of cutthroats remains hidden. *Library of Congress.*

concealment, board the hapless vessel and dispatch the crew with close-quarter weapons as quickly as possible.

Rachel's crew was credited with taking twelve ships and $12,000 in plunder and violently murdering twenty-four seafarers whose last moments were spent believing they were coming to the aid of a frightened woman.

The predations of Rachel and her gang reportedly came to an end during a storm in 1782, when the *Essex* herself was lost to the sea. According to some reports, Rachel's husband, George, died in the storm. Other reports indicate he simply left her. In any case, Rachel returned to Boston, where she continued her life of crime, specializing in nighttime burglaries aboard ships in the harbor but instinctively committing any crime of opportunity.

According to her own confession, given before her execution in 1789 and duly recorded as "taken from the prisoner's mouth, a few hours before her execution," by Deputy-Goaler Joseph Otis, Rachel takes credit for two such burglaries. How she was able to board these vessels without being discovered is still unclear. It may also be noteworthy that Rachel was not exactly the ideal witness, and so therefore her version of the events may be subject to the reader's own interpretation.

In 1787, Rachel recalled "she happened to go onboard" a ship tied up at Long Wharf in Boston, adding, "The Captain's name I cannot recollect, but think he was a Frenchman." At some point, she found herself, "entering the cabin, the door of which not being fastened, and finding the Captain and Mate asleep in their beds." Rachel said she "hunted about for plunder, and discovered, under the Captain's head, a black silk handkerchief containing upwards of thirty pounds, in gold, crowns, and small change, on which I immediately seized the booty and decamped therewith as quick as possible." Like any good pirate, Rachel was quick and merry with her newfound wealth. "I spent freely in company as wicked as myself, fully proving the old adage, 'light come light go,'" Rachel said.

In another incident, occurring in 1788, according to Rachel, "I broke into a sloop, on board of which I was acquainted, lying at Doane's Wharf." Rachel testified that she found "the Captain and every hand on board asleep in the cabin and steerage." The female outlaw must have been as stealthy as cat. "I looked round to see what I could help myself to, when I espied a silver watch hanging over the Captain's head, which I pocketed." Stealing a ticking watch from right over a sleeping seaman's head is the practice of someone who is either very skilled, very lucky, or both.

"I also took a pair of silver buckles out of the Captain's shoes." Rachel said, adding, "I likewise made free with a parcel of small change for pocket-money, to make myself merry among my evil companions, and made my escape without being discovered."

It may be noteworthy that Rachel, according to her own description, was already familiar with both vessels and apparently some of the crew. The captain on the first ship would have given no hint that he was a Frenchman while he was fast asleep. She must have had some sort of previous experience with him. In the second incident, she described the sloop as one with "which I was acquainted."

Finding one's way in the dark through unfamiliar hatches and passageways on any ship would certainly lead to inadvertent noises loud enough wake a slumbering sailor. This would indicate that Rachel had actually been aboard these vessels prior to her felonious acts. Perhaps even more intriguing is the deep sleep that these sailors were enjoying as their belongings were being spirited away, the kind of repose that would be enhanced with the immediate and previous consumption of alcoholic beverages. Since Rachel seemed to enjoy a merry lifestyle, had she been making merry with these sailors, aboard these very ships, perhaps the same night of the burglaries?

Rachel's confession, written before she was hanged for forcibly robbing a woman of a bonnet valued at seven shillings, may help clarify another issue—not with what is included in the document, but with what is not.

In a 2017 blog post, writer Amy Berkley rightfully brought into question the popular and well-published belief that Rachel Wall had in fact been a pirate plundering ships through deception around Isles of Shoals, as previously described in this chapter. Berkeley noted that Rachel hadn't described any tales of ocean piracy in her confession.

The tales of Rachel's seafaring adventures were first reported in 1959 by Edward Rowe Snow in his book *Piracy, Mutiny, and Murder* and picked up by other publications and websites through the years. According to Berkley, the source for this information is generally cited as the Robert Treat Paine Papers, a huge collection of documents maintained by the Massachusetts Historical Society. The files primarily include the papers of Robert Treat Paine, a Massachusetts lawyer, politician, member of the First Continental Congress, signer of the Declaration of Independence and justice of the Massachusetts Supreme Judicial Court who was active in the late 1700s until his death in 1814. The collection also includes documents from other family members, including well-known Revolutionary War patriot Thomas Paine, all of it filling nineteen reels of microfilm. The phrase needle in a haystack immediately comes to mind when considering confirmation of Rachel Wall's small-time activities in so ponderous a collection of history.

It should also be noted that Snow seemed to be in the habit of listing his bibliography entries in a general manner and that in the book *Piracy, Mutiny, and Murder*, the only mention of Robert Treat Paine is on page 61, describing him in his role as a prosecuting attorney in a case unrelated to Rachel Wall. A keyword search of the Paine Papers also reveals only one entry for "pirate," a council minutes "respecting two pirates apprehended at Machias" on July 21, 1785. This is an area far north of Isles of Shoals and predating Rachel Wall's reported pirate career.

So, it is not clear if the Paine Papers were the specific source for Rowe's information.

Nonetheless, Berkley undertook what must have been a time-consuming search of Paine's trial minutes from 1785 to 1789 concerning Rachel Wall and found no mention of her, bringing Berkley to the conclusion that "either the source has been cited incorrectly, or the tale of Rachel Wall [as a seafaring pirate] is just that—a tale."

While Berkley's efforts in pursuit of the truth are admirable, well intentioned and professional, they do rely on just one source, according to the information posted: the Robert Treat Paine Papers. And of course, Rachel Wall was never charged with or put on trial for piracy. So, it is possible that the Paine Papers were not Snow's source.

There is only one source that can be well confirmed, and that takes us back to Rachel Wall's own confession, made in the hours before her death with no apparent advantage for untruth, attested to by Rachel herself. She was already guilty of what was then a capital crime and sentenced to death, so why would she be less than truthful?

A better question might be, if she sought a sort of absolution for her wrongdoings, why would she be less than complete in her own recollection of her criminal career?

Perhaps the most probable explanation is the most obvious. Rachel had a long criminal career, and likely all of it wouldn't fit in to her confession.

Another explanation, especially for omitting her crimes of piracy, is even simpler. That explanation comes in the form of a human-shaped steel cage and the practice of gibbeting, a special means of execution for pirates during the late 1700s. Sometimes the bodies of previously hanged pirates would be put on public display, held erect by the confines of the steel cage, exposed to the weather, slowly decomposing and subject to the attention of passing birds and insects. In an even nastier application of this method, a live victim would be placed in the cage, put on display and left to die from thirst in full public view in a practice known as "sun drying." An illustration of gibbeting may be found in this book on page 43.

While this practice was performed with the purpose of deterring piracy, it may have also deterred Rachel Wall from a full confession. If she had confessed to piracy, then she might have been gibbeted like a pirate. Perhaps the notorious Rachel Wall held on to some of her secrets, favoring instead the common robber's fate of a quick death with a neck snap from the impact of a hangman's noose. Once the trapdoor on the gallows had been released under her feet, followed by a short drop into darkness, eternity and the unlikely possibility of spiritual absolution, Rachel knew that her eternity would at least begin with a decent burial, even if it would be in some forlorn patch of a pauper cemetery. Better that fate, Rachel likely thought, than decomposing in public view within the confines of a steel cage.

10

PIRATE WEAPONS AND TACTICS

Unlike the swashbucklers seen sword fighting to the death in many motion pictures, most actual pirates were quite content to avoid any real combat. Since their ultimate goal was usually the capture of coin, or cargo they could trade for coin, their overall strategy was relatively simple—get the goods, with minimum risk to themselves.

Still, a certain level of threat was required to accomplish this goal, and with threat comes the requirement to carry it out if need be, so weapons and tactics were requirements for these sea bandits

Pirates who frequented Maine shores from the late 1600s to the early 1700s brought with them types of weapons and tactics common with their brethren worldwide. Ubiquitous among these weapons was the pirate sword. Two types of swords were most popular with pirates during the period outlined, each with many variations and with the type of sword having much to do with the person using it.

Swordfighters with training or experience could enjoy the advantages of longer, elegant weapons, like the rapier, with a slim steel blade well sharpened on both edges extending over three feet from the hilt and tipped with a vicious point. (There were also smaller versions of rapiers known as short swords.) These were gentlemen's weapons generally carried by noblemen and officers. A well-trained user could deploy the long blade to keep an opponent at bay, perhaps far enough away so that if his adversary were using a shorter edged weapon he would be beyond range of striking the rapier swordfighter.

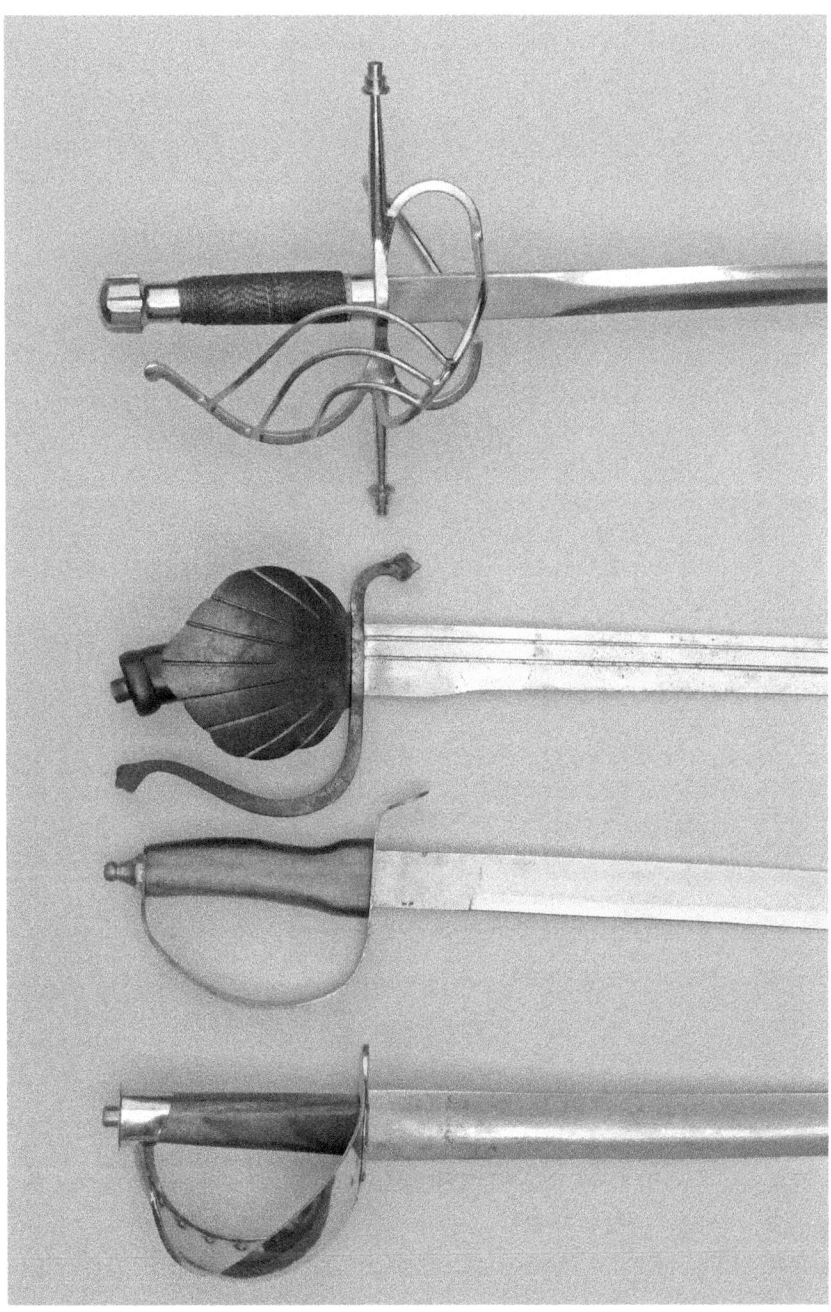

Hilts from the types of swords used by pirates in the late 1600s and early 1700s include (*from top to bottom*): a guarded hilt from a rapier, a clamshell guard on a cutlass hilt, a basic hand guard on a cutlass hilt and an enhanced steel hand guard on a cutlass. *George and Joanie Grey collection.*

Despite the long, double-edged blade, the rapier was not intended as a slashing weapon but instead a thrusting weapon, with the user capable of bringing the fight to a quick end by finding an opening in his antagonist's defense and deftly driving the blade point home through the enemy's chest, or using a quick turn of the wrist to slice open the opponent's neck. Unlike movie scenes filmed on elegant sets, with acrobatic swordsmen swinging from curtains and leaping from stairways, sometimes locking their weapons together as they stare each other down, real swordfighters strived for a quick and happy (for the winner) ending to combat.

Rapiers were also equipped with advantages found on the sword hilt (handle). Standard among these was a strong crosspiece designed to keep the adversary's weapon from sliding down the rapier blade to the user's hand. These swords usually included a knuckle bow that would curve from the lower front to the back of the grip, offering the user additional protection for his hand. Some models of rapiers offered cup hilts, with a cylindrical, bell-shaped barrier in front of the crosspiece designed to deflect a sword edge sliding down the rapier blade or to block an adversary's thrust at the rapier user's extended sword hand.

Key to the efficient use of the rapier was the grip on the sword hilt, which was often fashioned of wood or animal skin and wrapped with strands of leather or wire to prevent it from slipping in the swordfighter's hand. Although seemingly a small detail, the grip was a key part of the sword, as sweating hands and flowing blood could cause the weapon to slide out of the user's control if it wasn't properly built.

Lastly, a pommel would secure the end of the hilt, counterbalancing the sword and deadly when brought to bear in a smashing move to the opponent's head.

The rapier was beautiful to behold, so well balanced that the weight of the blade could barely be discerned, deadly in the hands of an experienced user and very expensive, therefore unavailable to many pirates except as a captured prize. While its length provided a great advantage in most environments, it was a major disadvantage aboard a ship, where rigging hangs low over the areas topside and confines are narrow in the 'tween decks. Therefore, it was another type of sword that was most often used by sea rovers, the cutlass.

Short, broad and cheap, the cutlass was an ugly cousin to the rapier's elegance. Moreover, using the weapon was essentially instinctive, and it could be successfully deployed immediately by anyone, regardless of experience or training. However, in the hands of an experienced user, the cutlass was quick and deadly.

Pirates and Lost Treasure of Coastal Maine

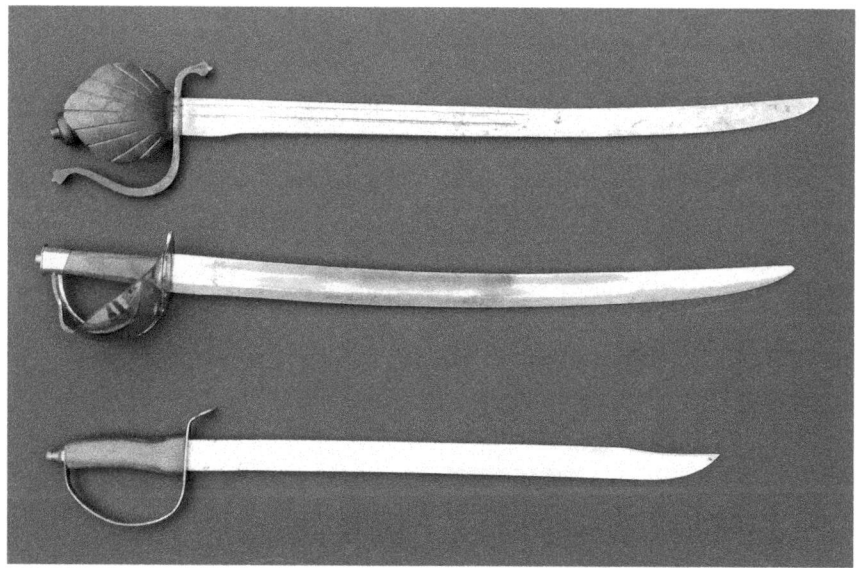

Full-length cutlasses used by pirates in the late 1600s and early 1700s include (*from top to bottom*): a cutlass featuring the popular clamshell guard, a cutlass with an enhanced steel hand guard and a cutlass with a basic hand guard. *George and Joanie Grey collection.*

Cutlass construction basics were simple, with the trademark being the stout blade, sharpened only on one side, sometimes with the blade growing thicker moving up from the sharpened edge for added strength. The blade was sometimes curved, making for easier slicing, or it could be left straight, making for easier construction. The sword was robust enough to serve a variety of purposes outside of combat. On board, the weapon could cut away ropes and sail canvas or could hack away at wood. On shore they could cut a path through heavy brush or thick jungle, and there is much speculation that the machete was developed from the cutlass.

The cutlass hilt came in many forms, depending on the owner's preferences or what style was available. At its most basic, there was usually a knuckle bow that would also serve as a crosspiece where it passed the base of the blade, extending far enough beyond the top of the blade to provide a stopping point if the user's hand slid up the grip or if an opponent's blade came down the top of the user's cutlass.

A more intricate design included a hand guard made to resemble either a single clam shell on one side of the hilt or double clam shells on either side of the hilt, functioning much like the cup hilt of a rapier. Another version of the hilt involved a large, robust guard that surrounded the user's hand with solid steel.

For pirates, the most attractive aspect of the cutlass, regardless of artistic design aspects, was its capability in combat. The weapon was deadly in close-quarter battle, using any combination of slash or stab techniques with the blade, punching with a metal hand guard or knuckle bow and pounding with the end of the pommel.

In an unusual demonstration of swordplay immortalized in pirate history, a woman bested her male counterparts at least twice in combat that likely involved some version of the cutlass.

Long before she sailed the seas, English-born Mary Read spent most of her lifetime disguised as a man. She had joined the British military and found herself assigned to the cavalry, where she would have been trained in techniques of the saber sword commonly used by mounted forces. Read was an exemplary cavalry recruit, rose to the rank of corporal and saw action in battle several times. While the cavalry saber she wielded would have been longer than a cutlass, it shared many similarities: a curved blade sharpened only on one edge with a hilt that usually included a hand guard.

After her military service ended (and after a marriage to her former cavalry tent-mate that ended when he died of disease), Read resumed her manly masquerade, this time as a sailor. When her ship was taken by the pirate captain Calico Jack Rackham in the early 1700s, she engaged the boarding pirates with her sword, holding three of them at bay for some time before Calico Jack intervened, wisely offering her a position with his crew before somebody got hurt. She decided to join Rackham's gang, still concealing her true gender, until she found herself in a duel with a male pirate. Her cavalry training once again paid off, and she was able to defeat her opponent in a sword fight, ripping away the front of her shirt as he lay dying, revealing her breasts so that he would know he had been killed by a woman.

The story of Mary Read reveals how training and experience can make all the difference between opponents when both are wielding the same type of edged weapon.

A swordfight to the death on a Maine island, with both fighters wielding similar weapons, is described in the ballad "The Slaying of Dixey Bull," found on pages 20–23 in chapter 3. The text describes Dixie's weapon as a "broadsword," a type of long double-edged sword with a wide blade and a basket hilt that generally predates the Golden Age of Pirates from the late 1600s to the early 1700s. However, Bull was active in the 1630s, so this description may be accurate, or it may inaccurately describe a cutlass. Either way, while the ballad is fanciful, the description of sword combat appears to be fairly accurate and may be of interest to the reader. (The term *broadsword* also refers to an earlier long blade two-handed sword, without a basket hilt, used in the Middle Ages.)

Firearms were also an important part of the sea rover's armory, and these weapons were experiencing a rapid progression in development just prior to and during the Golden Age of Piracy.

All of these arms worked around a system that involved an explosive and a projectile packed into a barrel, combined with an ignition system that, when activated, discharged the explosive and propelled the projectile out of the barrel—hopefully striking the intended target. This system is in many ways the same as a modern cartridge, with a primer to ignite a powder charge upon activation of the weapon trigger, discharging the bullet. What is today incorporated in a single cartridge was incorporated into the entire weapon, which had to be laboriously loaded by hand for every shot.

This process began with pouring a measured amount of explosive—in this era, black powder—into the barrel. Then the projectile, generally a round lead ball, would be inserted into the barrel, and a ramrod would be used to tamp the projectile down into the barrel, "seating" the ball firmly on the charge, leaving no space between the powder and the ball. Shooters with the time and equipment might have also had a small, square, lightly lubricated section of cloth to place under the ball, which would wrap around the projectile a bit as it was rammed home. In some cases, once the weapon was loaded, a small wad of cloth or paper may have been tamped down on top of the charge to secure it, especially if the weapon was being loaded well in advance of firing.

The next step depended on the type of firing system the weapon utilized, a hardware combination usually located on the right rear side of the gun called a "lock." These locks were under continuous development during the pirate era, and sea rovers would always seek the latest model they could find, or steal. Lock systems were applicable to either handguns or long guns.

Common to all lock systems was a flash pan, into which the shooter would deposit a small measure of powder, connected to the charge in the barrel through a touch hole.

Buccaneers operating in the early 1600s would have depended on one of the earliest lock systems, the matchlock. This system utilized a slow-burning fuse affixed in the "hammer" that was lowered on to the flash pan once the weapon was activated using either a standard trigger pull system or one activated by a lever.

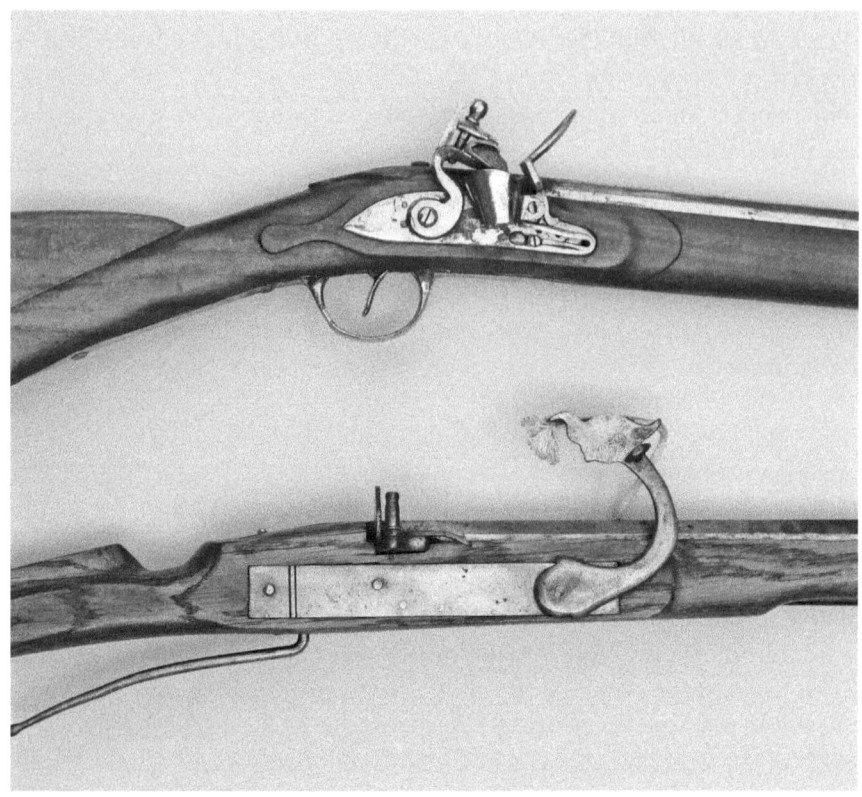

Early and advanced long gun lock systems, with the advanced flintlock system on top and the early matchlock system below. *George and Joanie Grey collection.*

These systems were state-of-the-art when first introduced in the mid-1400s but required extremely cumbersome barrels and stocks. The fuse could also become problematic if for any reason it couldn't be kept burning. While these weapons went out of style as soon as more efficient locks were developed, they remained in use with some cultures until relatively modern times. When the Chinese Red Army invaded Tibet in October 1950, they were met with fusillades from matchlock-wielding defenders. While the Tibetans were forced to capitulate to the much stronger Chinese forces during that battle, matchlocks remain in use for hunting among nomads in the Tibetan wilds.

Also in use during the 1600s was the wheellock system, which was the first self-igniting weapon, using a pyrite rock affixed to the weapon hammer to strike a spark near the flash pan—a much easier alternative to the burning fuse.

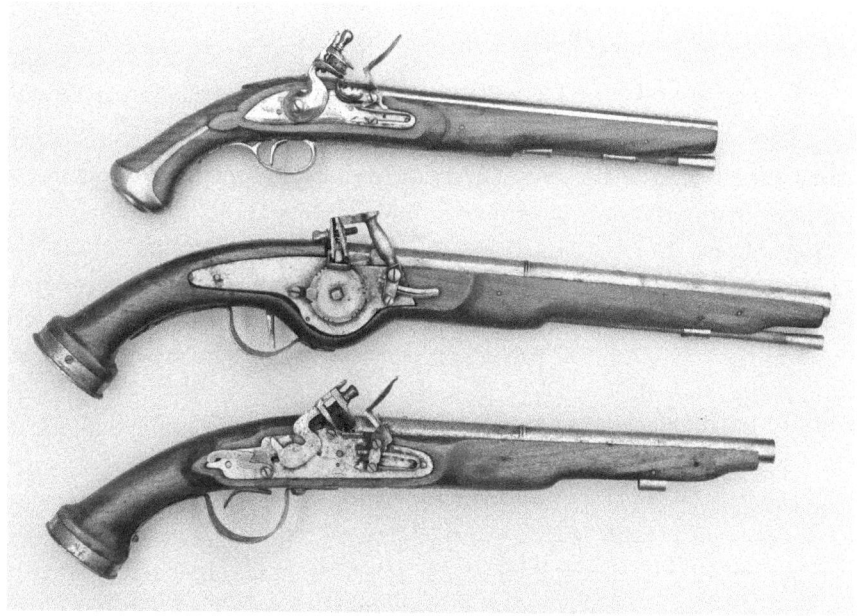

Three historic firearm lock systems *(from top to bottom)*: flintlock, wheel ock and doglock. *George and Joanie Grey collection.*

The next step up, first appearing in the mid-1600s, was the doglock, so called because an external catch mechanism called a "dog" was used to hold the hammer back once the weapon was cocked. These weapons featured a new ignition concept that utilized a flint affixed to the hammer of the weapon to strike a steel plate called a frizzen, simultaneously creating a spark and forcing open the cover to the flash pan, igniting the powder there and discharging the weapon. The doglock remained in fairly widespread use until the 1720s.

The final step in this arms race (at least through the 1700s) was the flintlock, which utilized the same ignition system as the doglock for discharging the weapon but included an interior locking mechanism that allowed the user to place the weapon on half cock, from which it could not be triggered accidentally (hence the phrase "don't go off half cocked"), or on full cock, from which the weapon could triggered. This made the gun much safer to load and carry.

All of these locks could work for handguns or long guns of the period, with wheellocks being exceptionally heavy if used on handguns.

Pirates utilized both handguns and long guns, but handguns were by far their preference. Easily portable, whether making landfall or forcibly boarding a ship, the handgun offered a powerful offensive weapon at close quarters and a frightening deterrent to those who might yet be undecided about resisting. As evidenced from many historic illustrations, pirates carried as many pistols as they could. With the weapons only good for one shot, the more pistols at hand, the more firepower immediately available as soon as required. Some illustrations show buccaneers with a brace (usually meaning two) of pistols fastened to either end of a cord or ribbon and worn straddling the neck, with a gun on either side. This rig allowed the user easy access to both of his weapons, and once discharged, the firearm could simply be dropped, still retained by the user by the attached ribbon. There are some depictions of pirates carrying four pistols this way. While this style of fast draw was historically illustrated, it was confirmed during Barry Clifford's underwater excavation of Sam Bellamy's flagship, the *Whydah*, off Wellfleet, Massachusetts. Among the artifacts recovered was a flintlock pistol with one end of a ribbon tied off on the rear part of the trigger guard, indicating it had been attached. (The other half had been separated after over two hundred years underwater.) This pistol has been on display at the Whydah Pirate Museum in Massachusetts and may be still be part of the displays there.

Many models of pistols used by pirates included a metal extension that ran from the back of the trigger guard down along the underside of the butt, which gave the weapon capability to block sword strokes. Once the pistol had fired the one shot it was made for, it would usually become a club; it could also stop a sword stroke in mid-swing. By transferring the spent firearm to the left hand and wielding the short cutlass in his right hand with the hilt near his waistline, a combatant could block the sword blade with the pistol handle by extending his left hand up and out. This maneuver would leave the opponent in the unfortunate position of (usually) having his right arm up with his blade stopped by the pistol, leaving his body completely open to a sudden upward thrust with the cutlass point to his center mass, ending in death or immobilization.

For those unfamiliar with the use of a flintlock pistol as a weapon other than a firearm, the technique is well documented in a popular movie, *The Patriot*, starring Mel Gibson, released in 2000.

While handguns had many advantages, especially in close-quarter battle, long guns had their own advantages and a unique place in pirate history.

Many people are familiar with the term *buccaneer* as another name for pirate, but the word actually began as unique to sea rovers of the early 1600s who were operating on the island of Hispaniola, the present-day

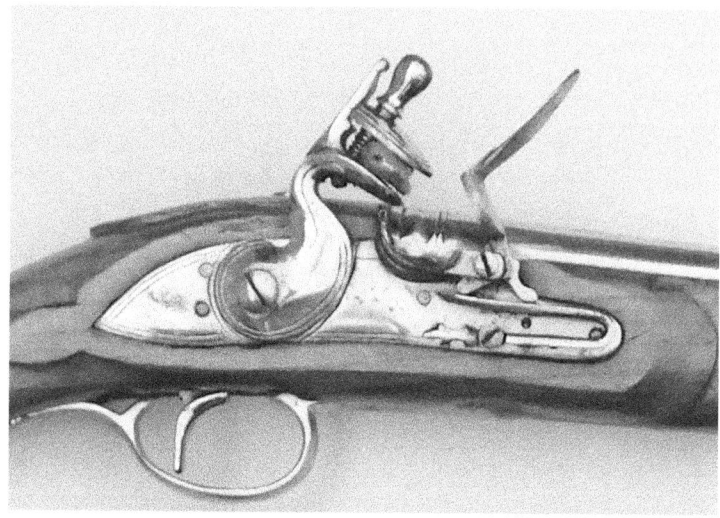

Detail of a flintlock pistol system. *George and Joanie Grey collection.*

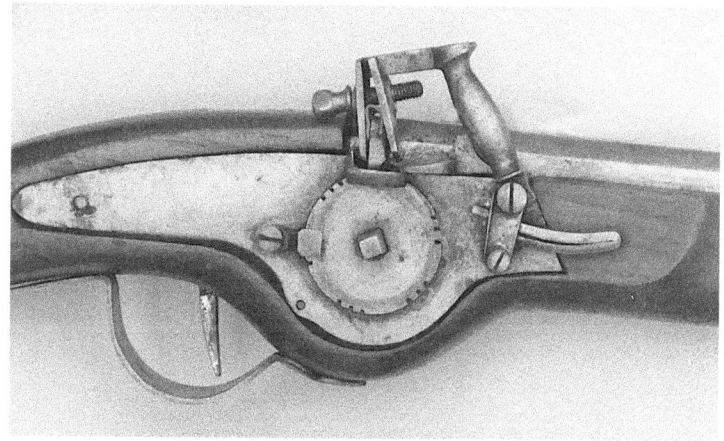

Detail of a wheellock pistol system. *George and Joanie Grey collection.*

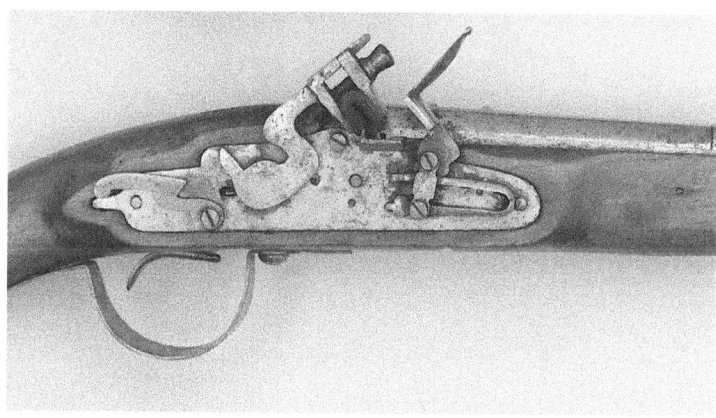

Detail of a doglock pistol system. *George and Joanie Grey collection.*

Dominican Republic and Haiti. These men, mostly of French descent, were interlopers on the island, which was ostensibly under Spanish control. Although the Spaniards fielded patrols, including mounted lancers, the island was simply too large to successfully secure. Armed with muskets, these French interlopers would hunt for livestock the Spaniards had left behind on the island, dressing their kills out and smoking the meat on greenwood frames used by indigenous people called *buccans*. This term evolved into a French word, *boucane*, and these men became known as *boucaniers*, Anglicized as *buccaneer*, which was later adapted to describe almost any pirate. These early boucaniers were able to make a somewhat honest living, selling the dried meat from their boucanes to passing non-Spanish ships. Occasionally, they would also foray out into coastal waters using native wooden sailing canoes called periaguas (sometimes spelled piragua) to seek and surreptitiously board by night slow-moving merchant vessels, forcing the crew to surrender and taking whatever was of value.

These boucaniers became incredibly adept at marksmanship using their smoothbore muskets and lead round shot, a combination that would usually have very little accuracy, even at short distances. It is likely that they spent considerable effort ensuring the barrels on their weapons were as true as possible, fine-tuning the size of their shot so it fit the barrel diameter perfectly and adjusting the powder used to match the range and velocity desired for whatever target requirement they found themselves drawing a sight on.

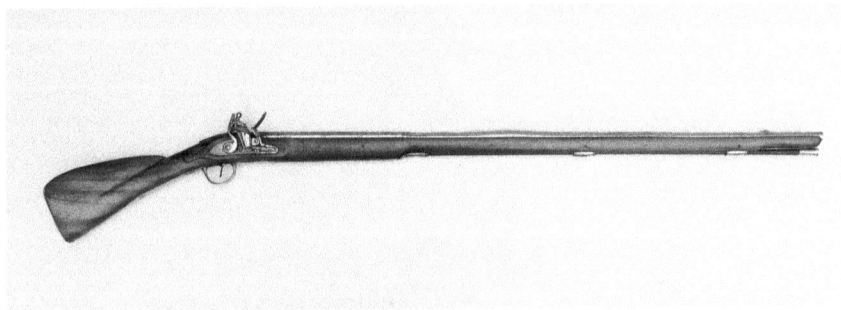

Pictured is a Charleville musket, widely used after being introduced as the standard French infantry firearm in 1717. While pirates used a variety of flintlock long guns, this version of the Charleville provides a good example of the weapon type. These guns were equipped with long, smoothbore barrels, muzzle-loaded with powder and ball, discharged using a flint on the weapon's hammer striking a steel frizzen and igniting powder in a flash pan, with the flame traveling though a touch hole into the base of the barrel and discharging the weapon. Some buccaneers were surprisingly accurate with these muskets. *George and Joanie Grey collection.*

Pirates and Lost Treasure of Coastal Maine

As the boucaniers became integrated into pirate crews, it was said that four sharp-shooting boucaniers, from a range of several hundred yards, were more useful than a cannon in keeping opposing crew from accessing a ship's deck. The use of small arms also had the added advantage that musketry couldn't accidentally sink a valuable ship and cargo, while a poorly aimed cannon shot could. Unlike their navy counterparts, pirates weren't looking to destroy their opponents, only to take their belongings as efficiently as possible, so it was to this end that the tactics they used were developed.

Again, the cinematic image of bloodthirsty buccaneers aboard a well-armed, full-sized square-rigged ship, blasting away with artillery, closing in on an equally large, treasure-laden Spanish galleon, is the popular image of a pirate sea battle. In fact, such a scenario would have been highly unlikely. The vessels preferred by buccaneers were usually small and fast. Single-masted sloops, small in size, shallow-drafted and faster than larger ships, were popular with sea rovers operating in the Caribbean. Crews requiring ships with longer ranges for plundering in West Africa and the Indian Ocean would seek somewhat larger vessels such as the three-masted bark favored by Bartholomew Roberts when he sailed the South Atlantic, whose adventures are documented on these pages in chapter 6.

On rare occasions, sea rovers would have the opportunity to take and refit larger vessels, preferring slave ships because of their speed and ease of use in battle with no interior bulkheads, allowing crew to move freely fore and aft in the 'tween decks, bringing ammunition to the guns. The best examples of captured, refitted slavers were the *Whydah* under Black Sam Bellamy and *Queen Anne's Revenge* under Blackbeard. Both of these ships were large and well armed enough to challenge even a Royal Navy fourth-rate ship of the line, about the same size as latter-day frigates such as the USS *Constitution*. If the *Queen Anne's Revenge* hadn't run aground prior to Blackbeard's final defeat in battle, taking it out of the fight, the outcome would have likely been entirely different.

Pirates were essentially armed sea robbers, and very much like most present-day armed robbers, they wanted to grab the goods and get away with as little effort and trouble as possible. With that being the case, they usually didn't want to sink any ships, at least not until they could plunder their holds. They also wanted to avoid combat and the possibility of casualties to themselves or the crew of their prey vessel. Any deaths construed to be murders would quickly bring a pirate ship and its crew to the attention of any nearby naval forces and the possibility of capture.

Pirates and Lost Treasure of Coastal Maine

Generally speaking, pirates used threats and intimidation to force their prey into capitulation. If the first element in engaging their prey was to frighten them into submission, the pirates used the first thing their victims would see, a flag hoisted atop one of the masts on their vessel. Often capture maneuvers would first involve a long pursuit, in slow motion by modern day standards, as one or more pirate vessels would locate and then slowly close distance, under sail, on a potentially lucrative merchant ship.

In order to make these pursuits shorter, pirates would often deploy a false flag to allay the fears of the merchant crew until the vessel being pursued was close enough for capture. If the buccaneers observed that the merchant ship was flying a flag designating a nationality, they might hoist the same type of flag or that of a nation they knew would be considered friendly by the merchant crew. It was common for all types of ships, including merchantmen, to carry a variety of flags to be utilized when needed. A good description of this practice, and the confusion it caused, may be found on these pages in chapter 4.

Once the range between the vessels was narrowed, the sea rovers would take the next step in terrifying the merchant crew by running up in their rigging a special ensign revealing their true intention.

These flags could be as simple as a plain black or red cloth, with the black generally meaning that the lives would be spared of those who surrendered without a fight and the red more ominously meaning "no quarter," so no lives would be spared.

As time went on, certain pirate captains created their own signature flags with trademark images on a black or red field. The so-called Jolly Roger, a white skull and crossbones on a black field, is the most generally recognized of these images. However, pirates could be creative with their logos, using arms with swords, hourglasses, hearts, full skeletons and even dancing figures, in many combinations, to personalize their ensigns.

Once the distance between ships was closed and the warning flag raised, the pirate's choice of intimidation methods became much more direct. If no hostile fire had yet been exchanged, the sea rovers would bring their vessel alongside the merchantman, and the heavily armed buccaneer crew would crowd the deck of their ship, waving weapons, shouting threats and running out artillery pieces from their ports. This tactic was known as vaporing.

There was a substantial difference in how commercial ships and pirate vessels were staffed. The owners of merchant ships wanted to save money by hiring as few crew members as possible, often fewer than a dozen. On the other hand, pirate captains welcomed as many sea rovers as they could fit on their vessel, ensuring plenty of hands if there was a fight and a better possibility of survivors if there were combat casualties or if disease struck the ship's company.

This simple difference in numbers, combined with the fact that merchant crews were hired to sail ships, not fight, usually resulted in a swift surrender. When it didn't, the marauders would step up the level of violence.

Naval guns could carry many types of loads, with the common cannonball being unpopular, as pirates were concerned of the possibility such ordnance might blast a hole in the target vessel, sinking it to the bottom of the sea with all the lovely treasure still aboard. Instead, they would load the guns with specialized projectiles. Chain shot, constructed with a length of chain fastened to heavy objects on either end, would be used to damage sails, masts and rigging to either slow a ship or bring it to a standstill. Grapeshot, hundreds of small caliber lead balls, or even a collection of nails or other steel objects, could transform the cannon into a huge shotgun that could decimate any crew on deck with a hail of projectiles.

Finally, the pirates would use grappling hooks and lines to pull the prey vessel alongside their ship and engage the remaining crew in bloody hand-to-hand combat. Fortunately for most merchant crews, and to the convenience of sea rovers, such a final scenario was rare.

Buccaneers were also perfectly capable of amphibious assault on land-based targets, generally relying on overwhelming force but in some cases capable of military discipline. When Captain Henry Morgan attacked Panama City in 1671, his buccaneers, many of them former soldiers, assaulted the fort in good order, divided into three columns.

Benerson Little, author of *The Sea Rover's Practice* and a former Navy SEAL, noted that pirates' ability to improvise, adapt and overcome demonstrated an "indomitable will in the best and worse of circumstances." In the final analysis, this willpower, combined with the right tactics and weapons—and more than a wee bit of luck and pluck—made piracy in the late 1600s and early 1700s a sometimes profitable, and sometimes deadly, method of making one's fortune.

11
PLENTY OF "PIRATITUDE" IN MODERN-DAY MAINE

While outlaw pirates are now relegated to Maine history, modern-day events and reenactments still honor both buccaneer traditions and the natural "piratitude" of the Pine Tree State.

Sports teams have followed the nautical theme, with names like Portland Pirates, Maine Mariners, Portland Sea Dogs and Maine Windjammers.

Dining and entertainment locations include Pirates Patio in Old Orchard Beach and Pirates Cove Adventure (Mini) Golf in Bar Harbor.

A walking excursion, hosted by Red Cloak Tours in several Midcoast Maine towns and led by a costumed interpreter, covers maritime history and mystery, including stories of pirates and treasure.

During the summer season in Maine, it is easy for any resident or visitor to relive the tales, see the action, hear the sounds of sword steel clashing, feel the reverberation of cannon fire and even catch the scent of freshly discharged gunpowder at any number of pirate-themed events. Both large and small, these events can range from hourlong speaking engagements to rollicking affairs lasting for days. While it is impossible to list all of these with accurate dates from year to year in this book, the most established events can certainly be included with general information for the reader to follow up on, although these events are subject to change.

Many of these occasions feature costumed reenactors, with one group, the Pirates of the Dark Rose, being the best known and most widely traveled in the state. Based in Camden, the Pirates of the Dark Rose are real sword-wielding, flintlock-brandishing reenactors who will get right into the action and bring audiences with them.

Pirates and Lost Treasure of Coastal Maine

Members of the Pirates of the Dark Rose showing off their "piratitude." *Author photo.*

At many coastal events, they sail in aboard their fifty-seven-foot yawl, armed with nine cannons and crewed by a gang of heavily armed cutthroats. On shore, they have emplacements for cannon and a pirate village that they set up. During the event, they engage in a wide variety of activities, from puppet shows to pirate parodies, all the way to arms demonstrations. Their cannon and firearms are working replicas, so demonstrations and actual use of the weapons during dramatic reenactments are commonplace. The Pirates of the Dark Rose also carry combat-quality swords and are trained to use them, so staged sword fighting is often part of the show.

Historical interpretation is also part of the range of activities offered by the Pirates of the Dark Rose, and key among these is the historic artifact exhibition curated by George Grey. Included with this display are actual pieces and authentic replicas of firearms, edged weapons, artillery ammunition and more, all available for the audience to examine while Grey provides a knowledgeable narrative.

The Pirates of the Dark Rose are usually associated with the following events: Windjammer Days in Boothbay Harbor, usually held in late June; Pirate Parlay at Fort Knox in Prospect, usually held in mid-July; and the

A group of reenactors with the Pirates of the Dark Rose involved in a sword battle during an event in Damariscotta, Maine. *Don Dunbar, easternmaineimages.com; Damariscotta Pirate Rendezvous.*

An artillerist with the Pirates of the Dark Rose discharges a field piece in the direction of pirate vessels approaching on the Damariscotta River. *Don Dunbar, easternmaineimages.com; Damariscotta Pirate Rendezvous.*

Windjammer Festival in Camden, usually held in late August/early September. There are a number of other events featuring the Pirates of the Dark Rose. Schedule information and more is available online at thepiratesofthedarkrose.com.

For late-season visitors to downeast Maine, the Eastport Pirate Festival offers three full days of rowdy pirate fun usually over a weekend in early September. This event is filled with a wide variety of lighthearted activities, including a Lobster Crate Race and a Kids Pirate Boat Ride, all highlighted with a street parade, a fireworks display and a Pirate Ball. There are many more activities in the schedule, and these may be checked online at eastportpiratefestival.com. Eastport is the easternmost city in the United States and the first city in the country to see the sunrise every morning.

Colonial Pemaquid in the town of Bristol is a state historic site, complete with an authentically rebuilt stone fort, actual building foundations left behind by the earliest settlers and a schedule of events focused on history. This is also the location, discussed earlier in this book (chapter 3, "Dixie

Pirates of all sizes can be seen advancing on the in-town area of Damariscotta during a past pirate event. *Don Dunbar, easternmaineimages.com; Damariscotta Pirate Rendezvous.*

Pirates and Lost Treasure of Coastal Maine

Pirate boats, led by the SV *Must Roos*, manned by Pirates of the Dark Rose, advance up the Damariscotta River during a pirate event. *Don Dunbar, easternmaineimages.com; Damariscotta Pirate Rendezvous.*

Bull, Maine's First Pirate"), where Dixie Bull raided in 1632. For more information on events, check friendsofcolonialpemaquid.org.

While the Maine Maritime Museum (mainemaritimemuseum.org) in Bath features permanent and changing exhibits of all things nautical, sometimes including sea bandits, there is always a buccaneer activity available for children—the Pirate Playship. A large, multilevel wooden climbing structure that looks like a galleon-style ship, the Pirate Playship is a kids' favorite located in an outdoor area on museum grounds and available all season. Of course, there are a multitude of other seafaring exhibits and hands-on activities that children and adults can both enjoy. Perhaps of additional note, Morse Cove in Phippsburg, where some of Black Bart Robert's treasure may still be buried (as described in chapter 6), is only a ten-minute drive from the museum. Part of that area, where the town landing is located, is easily accessible to the public. A paved, winding driveway, off Fiddlers Reach Road, takes visitors right to the shore. While any treasure will likely continue to remain lost in the ever-changing landscape, rocks with quartz-like encrustations, like the boulder described in the treasure map detailed in that chapter, are easy to find and small enough to make memorable souvenirs of pirate history and the tempting possibility of lost treasure in Maine.

BIBLIOGRAPHY

Berkley, Amy. "Pirate in a Petticoat: The Legend of Rachel Wall." History of Boston and Beyond. robertallisonhistory.wordpress.com.
Brophy, Jessica. "History Channel Films in Stonington." *Island Ad-Vantages* (Stonington, ME), July 31, 2014.
Brown, Charlotte Beath. *In Old Boothbay: The Brick House and Other Stories*. Boothbay Harbor, ME: Boothbay Register Press, 1926.
Burgess, Douglas R., Jr. *The Pirates' Pact*. New York, NY. McGraw Hill, 2009.
Champernowne, Captain Francis, and Charles Wesley Tuttle. *The Dutch Conquest of Acadie*. Boston: John Wilson & Son, University Press, 1889.
Chase, Fanny S. *Wiscasset in Pownalborough*. Portland, ME. Anthoenson Press, 1967.
Colavito, Jason. "Review of *America Unearthed* S03E06 'Captain Kidd's Pirate Code.'" December 13, 2014. jasoncolavito.com, 2014.
Cordingly, David. *Under the Black Flag: The Romance and Reality of Life among the Pirates*. New York: Random House, 2006.
Crooker, William S. *Pirates of the North Atlantic*. Halifax, NS: Nimbus Publishing, 2004.
Di Vece, Phil. "Captain Kidd's Pot of Gold Wasn't at the Rainbow's End." *Wiscasset (ME) Newspaper* October 19, 2015.
Dow, George Francis, and John Henry Edmonds. *Pirates of the New England Coast*. New York: Dover Publications, 1996.
Eckstom, Fannie, and Mary W. Smyth. *Minstrelsy of Maine*. New York: Houghton Mifflin, 1927.

Bibliography

Edmonds, John Henry. *Captain Thomas Pound*. Cambridge, MA: John Wilson & Son University Press, 1918.

Girard, Geoffrey. *Tales of the Atlantic Pirates*. Moorestown, NJ: Middle Atlantic Press, 2006.

Gosse, Philip. *The Pirates' Who's Who*. Glorietta, NM: Rio Grande Press, 1924.

Head, Franklin H. "Olmsted and Captain Kidd's Treasure." *Liberty Magazine*, 1934.

———. "Shakespeare's Insomnia and the Causes Thereof." Project Gutenberg, gutenberg.org.

———. *Studies in American History: A Notable Lawsuit*. Chicago: privately printed, 1887.

Hull, John T. *The Siege and Capture of Fort Loyall*. Portland, ME: Owen, Strout & Company, 1885.

Jameson, John Franklin. *Privateering and Piracy in the Colonial Period*. New York: J.J. Little & Ives Company, 1923.

Jameson, W.C. *Buried Treasure of New England*. Little Rock, AR: August House, 1998.

———. *Buried Treasures of the Atlantic Coast*. Little Rock, AR: August House, 1998.

Johnson, Charles. *A General History of the Robberies and Murders of the Most Notorious Pyrates*. London: Conway Maritime Press, 1998. (Original published in 1724. Actual author(s) are likely Daniel Defoe, Nathaniel Mink and possibly others.)

Jones, Herbert G. *I Discover Maine: Little Known Stories about a Well-Known State*. Portland, ME: Machigonne Press, 1937.

Lavery, Brian. *The Ship of the Line*. Bloomsbury, UK: Conway Maritime Press, 2003.

Little, Benerson. *The Sea Rover's Practice: Pirate Tactics and Techniques*. Washington, D.C.: Potomac Books, I2005.

Matos, Raimundo Jose de Cunha. *Corographia Historica das Ilhas de S. Tome, Principe, Ano Bom e Fernando Po*. São Tomé: Imprenesa Nacional, 1916.

Members of the Phippsburg Historical Society. *Phippsburg—Fair to the Wind*. Lewiston, ME: Penmor Lithographers, 1995.

Nelson, James L. "Piracy and the Coast of Maine." mainecrimewriters.com.

———. *The Pirate Round*. New York: Harper Collins/Perrenial, 2001.

Nelson, Laura. "Peter Cornelius Hoof and Me." The Whydah Pirates Speak, petercornelius.blogspot.com.

———. "Sam Bellamy and Oliver Levasseur—Two Pirates Just Kickin' Around the Caribbean." Pirates and Privateers. http://cindyvallar.com.

BIBLIOGRAPHY

———. *The Whydah Pirates Speak*. N.p., Postillion LLC, 2016.
Pascal Bonenfant. pascalbonenfant.com.
Piatt, Walter E., Major. "The Attack on Panama City by Henry Morgan." Master's thesis, Fort Leavenworth, KS, U.S. Army Command and General Staff College, 1998.
Pirate Documents. "Bartholomew Roberts' Death 1722." piratedocuments.com.
Sanders, Richard. *If a Pirate I Must Be…The True Story of Black Bart*. New York: Sky Horse Publishing, 2007.
Seitz, Don C. *Under the Black Flag: Exploits of the Most Notorious Pirates*. Mineola, NY: Dover Publications, 2001.
Sewall, Rufus King. *Ancient Dominions of Maine*. Bath, ME: Elisha Clark and Company, 1859.
Snow, Edward Rowe. *Piracy, Mutiny and Murder*. New York: Dodd, Mead and Company, 1959.
———. *Pirates and Buccaneers of the Atlantic Coast*. Beverly, MA: Commonwealth Editions, 2004.
Stevens, C.J. *The Buried Treasures of Maine*. Phillips, ME: John Wade, Publisher, 1997.
Trinity Church Wall Street. "Captain Kidd Lends Runner & Tackle for Building First Trinity Church." trinitywallstreet.org.
Tuttle, Charles Wesley. *Capt. Francis Champernowne, The Dutch Conquest of Acadie*. Boston: University Press, 1889.
Wilbur, Keith C. *Pirates and Patriots of the Revolution*. Old Saybrook, CT: Globe Pequot Press, 1972.
Willis, William. "Coins Found on Richmond Island, Maine." *American Journal of Numismatics* 5, no. 2 (1870).
Woodard, Colin. *Ayuh, Ye Mateys! Did the Pirates of the Caribbean Build a Lair in Down East Maine?* Portland, ME: Portland Press Herald, 2012.
———. *The Republic of Pirates*. New York: Harcourt, 2007.
Zacks, Richard. *The Pirate Hunter*. New York: Hyperion Special Markets, 2002.

ABOUT THE AUTHOR

Author Greg Latimer in character as the pirate "Scribe." *Author's collection.*

Greg Latimer has been separating fact from fiction since he first started as a newspaper reporter at the age of sixteen, and he continues to do so with this latest book.

By age eighteen, he was a full-time reporter/photographer for a newspaper in Los Angeles. It was only several years later that he moved up to the position of investigative reporter for the daily *Los Angeles Herald Examiner*, where he established his reputation through coverage of the infamous torture-murders committed by Roy Lewis Norris and Lawrence Sigmund Bittaker.

His fact-based investigative reporting came to the attention of a detective lieutenant with the police department in Hermosa Beach, California (located in southwest Los Angeles County), and Latimer was recruited as a police evidence photographer. After some years there, he returned to journalism and eventually moved to Maine, where he was employed by the Lincoln County Publishing Company in Newcastle until his retirement in 2018. In 2001 he was recognized by the New England Press Association with an award for investigative reporting.

Latimer is the research director for MysteriousDestinationsMagazine.com, an online publication that explores mysteries in the United States and the Caribbean, and the marketing director for Red Cloak Tours in Maine, where he also guides maritime history tours.

Latimer has worked as a pirate reenactor in Maine, firing cannon and black powder small arms, participating in sword fights and sailing armed vessels, giving him a sense of piracy that is up close and personal. He continues to do speaking engagements as the pirate "Scribe," a character fashioned after a real sea rover, William Dampier, who circled the globe three times as a navigator aboard English ships seeking Spanish treasure.

His books *Haunted Damariscotta* and *Ghosts of the Boothbay Region* were previously published by The History Press/Arcadia Publishing.